CRYSTAL LAW

Luis Martinez

L M B

LUIS MARTINEZ BOOKS

CRYSTAL LAW

ISBN 9781733885751

Printed in USA

DEDICATION

I dedicate Crystal Law to my best friend, Alvin Young. You came into my life at a time when I needed it most. You taught me one of the best lessons that I truly feel helped save my life; walk away from situations that would only end in violence or with negative consequences. You always said, "The bigger man who walks away will always be the person that wins because he gets to live another day." It was because of our conversations that I became inspired to write. I hated reading but one day you brought me a Donald Goines book to read. Once I finished reading it, I told myself that I too can write my own stories. You were the missing piece in my life. You taught me how to be a man, but most importantly, you took me off the streets and kept me alive.

Table of Contents

Sasa,

Thank you for all your support & most importantly for your friendship

Best of luck to you!!

LOVE Chino

NOTICE

Most people can't explain the moment in which their lives may have taken a turn for the worse. As for me, I can pretty much pinpoint mine. I can tell you how old I was and even where I was standing when that occurred. I may not have known it at the time, but looking back, I am almost 100% sure that it was the day that I saw that piece of paper that looked as if it had just been taken out of an envelope and placed on the refrigerator door with a magnet by my mother. All I remember seeing were those big red letters that spelled the word NOTICE followed by the words, child support. Now, although I had no idea what that meant exactly, I knew that if it was on the refrigerator door that it definitely had to be very serious. I knew that it was important because the only other things that were ever placed there were either bills or anything negative that was sent by our school. I didn't read the entire letter because I didn't really think anything of it at the time. So, I just carried on, went into the refrigerator, got what I needed and within a few minutes, forgot all about the letter.

Now, before I get into this introduction, I want to let all of you know that these thoughts go all the way back to the late 1980s. My views on life and the relationship between my parents and I have since changed. I am in a much better place mentally today than I was back then. I am now a father of two boys, Jerek and Jaxon, who both mean the world to me. But, dating back 30 years ago throughout my teens and early adult life, I must admit, I was completely out of control. I had no idea which way to go or who to turn to. I was only in my teens and I was ready to just give up on life. I turned to what I knew best at the time, the street life. Nothing in life seemed to have been working in my favor no matter how hard I tried. In fact, it seemed as though the harder I pushed myself to do better, the worse my situation seemed to become. I couldn't understand how after everything that I did to make everyone around me happy that it was not being viewed or accepted in ways that I believed and thought it should've been.

It really wasn't until I ended up in couples counseling in May of 2017 that it all began to make sense to me. At the time, it was my fiancé's idea that we seek professional help because she couldn't understand where all of my anger and frustration was coming from. I honestly believe that it was the best decision that I have ever made in my life. I literally poured my heart out in every session. No one has ever seen me cry as much as my counselor, Ms. Mary, and my fiancé did for about a month straight. It was tough, but it was well worth it and way overdue. I had been holding onto so much that the counselor brought me all the way back to the age of 12. I still remember her calling me a "man child" who was still stuck in his teenage years. It really pissed me off at the time.

One day, I was put under so much pressure by the both of them that I stormed out and just walked all the way home. I have been through a lot, but I believe that day was the most intense day that I had ever faced. For an entire week, I hated the both of them because they went against everything I said. After calming down and thinking things through, I realized then that there was something seriously wrong with me. I concluded that the way that I had been dealing with all of my issues in the past were now affecting me at home.

During those meetings, I was given the opportunity to speak freely without any interruptions. Any time one of us spoke out of turn, she would put her hand up to referee the session. The best part about the sessions was that I couldn't yell and curse like I had been used to doing during any of my arguments or disagreements that we had at home. It taught me how to handle my disputes differently and with a lot less anger. The sessions were held at a church about two miles down the road from our house. So, in place of all those curse words that I would have normally used to express my anger and frustration, I had to find a better way to say things. Only this time, I would be crying and choking up between words as I began to open up more and more about my past. But, what these counseling sessions did for me would have never been revealed anywhere else. As a matter of fact, I probably would have died holding onto all my stress and personal issues that I had been struggling with. I can't thank Ms. Mary enough for finally pushing me to opening up like I had never done before.

The session that took me back to that NOTICE placed on the refrigerator was the game changer and leads me to this. I want you to understand that I love my parents more than any words could ever describe. I have always loved my mom. But, growing up, my daddy was my superhero. He still is. It's crazy because my oldest son treats me the same way that I used to look up to my dad. I can almost go as far as to say that I was my daddy's favorite. I say that because I always wanted to go everywhere that he went and be by his side no matter what it was that he was doing. But eventually, that all changed drastically. Everything seemed to have fallen and broken into pieces once he saw that notice on the refrigerator. Soon after that, I began to see my dad seem more serious and a lot less happy.

He began hanging out more and coming home later. It broke my heart. And although I couldn't understand it then, I completely understand it now. My dad, like anyone else, was human and he made mistakes. Mistakes that almost caused a divorce between my parents and us having to grow up without our father. In fact, I remember my dad asking me in a whisper, "If your mom and I separated, who would you want to go with?" It was a tough question for me to answer. Not because of having to choose between the two, but because I couldn't understand how we got there from one day to the next. Everything was peaceful until that letter was posted on that refrigerator. I felt my dad's love for me shift and he became consumed with anger and self-hate. He became devil-like in my eyes. That changed everything. My parent's issues due to my dad having a daughter outside of their marriage changed my life. Till this day, I still have not met my sister, Lena. I have nothing against her, in fact, I can't wait to finally meet her one day.

Keep in mind though, good or bad, positive or negative, my dad was and still is my first role model. Besides all that I looked up to him for, things like taking me everywhere and showing me how to fish and spending real quality time with me, I also took in the bad. I started drinking, I couldn't stay faithful in any relationship that I ever got into, and I just wanted to stay out more, just to be like him. In fact, the same way that he became angry at the world, I too, began to feel the same way. I became rebellious.

Once I began to feel like I had no other choice than to try and find a way to fill that empty space that my parent's relationship had left in my heart, I found love where most would consider the worst place on earth. It was all right there in front of me. Right outside our 3rd floor window. For years, I had always remembered my dad telling us that while we played outside that we were to never ever walk into the building across from where we lived. That building was known to many as the C building. But, since things had changed at home, all that ever did for me was make me more curious. I became closer friends with the two kids that lived in the C building. Their names were Richie and Noel Morales. Richie or "Marv" as he called himself, was the first dealer that I ever met. I didn't know that he was a dealer when I first met him, but after a few weeks, all of that became very obvious to me. Their father was a maintenance supervisor at the Crystal Avenue apartments at the time and a close friend of my dad's. They played on the same softball team so that made it even easier for me to go over to their apartment every now and then. And, what I saw in the hallways that led up to their apartment (that I couldn't see from my 3rd floor window) was an entirely different world. It's hard to explain what really attracted me to what I saw, but in a few words, I just wanted in.

All it took was a few minutes for me to see what was going on in those hallways to understand why my dad was so adamant about warning us not to go into that building. Being that I was only allowed to play on the concrete or at the park because it was in plain view of our window, all I really knew at the time were just a few names. Some of my friends were always mentioning names like DeJohn Strong (RIP), Merrill Epps (RIP) and Richie Morales (RIP). According to my friends, they were the ones making most of the money that came through those hallways. It was at that very moment that I decided that I needed to get closer to Richie in order to find out what this drug dealing thing was all about.

Once my friends began noticing that I was no longer playing football or baseball with them anymore, they knew what I had gotten myself into. The changes in my life came just that quick and were obvious to those who knew me best. Looking back, I believe that it was a crazy decision for me to make, but at that time, of course it felt like it was the best choice for me. I was tired of looking different from all the rest. Everyone had new sneakers and clothes, and they seemed to be enjoying life more. And, most importantly, they didn't have a care in the world about what was going on outside of the projects. Crystal Avenue was our world.

I made the adult decision to sell drugs by the age of 12. Almost overnight, I went from being a straight A student and an All-Star baseball player to a petty drug dealer as I have mentioned previously in my books Loser and Lie'f. The love that I no longer felt coming from my dad was now coming from the drug dealers that I quickly embraced and that took me in. It was a different kind of love, but at least I felt they cared. Well, at least they acted like they did. Occasionally, the dealers would ask me why I chose to hang out with them instead of continuing to follow my dreams of becoming a professional baseball player. My response to them was that it was my dad's dream and it was no longer mine. My heart was not into playing baseball anymore. All I wanted to do was hang out, make money, and no longer feel or deal with the pain from what was going on at home. I got so caught up with becoming a crook that I began taking my dad's beers and chugging them in the hallway and even went in his pockets to steal his money while he took a nap. I had become a criminal in my own mind, and it really made me feel like I was feeding that empty space so much that it began to feel like I was living a double life. The good in me was being poisoned and overpowered by all the negative things that I was learning at such a fast pace that I created my own path straight to hell on earth.

My decision to hang out in the streets and to sell drugs was a decision that at the time felt like the right one, but I must admit that until this day, I am still affected in many ways from the things that I saw and the negative things that I personally did. Once I was accepted by my street peers as being one of them, I lost all my motivation and interest to do anything positive that my dad had tried to get us to do. Once I was chest deep into the streets, I started being called a Loser by those that used to know me as a good kid. But, I just didn't care. My life was heading in an entirely different direction from those that I used to consider my closest friends.

I can still remember the first time I ever walked into the C building. All I saw was a bunch of black kids smoking weed and drinking 40's of Old English beer while rolling dice and crack fiends coming in and out the doors. The way they all stood around laughing and telling jokes wasn't the only thing that caught my attention. It was the way they all dressed that made me feel like I needed to start making money myself. I was tired of the hand-me-downs. I was tired of being laughed at by my friends for the way I dressed compared to them. So, I started as a "look out" kid and began making a few dollars here and there. It felt great not having to ask my parents for anything or having to steal my dad's money. The best part though, I was no longer being laughed at for wearing fake Jordan's from Payless anymore. I would rush to go to sleep just so the morning would hurry up and come in order to catch the early bird crackheads. The more I hung out and dealt drugs, the better I got at it. So much so that I had to start lying to my parents by telling them that different girls were buying all my outfits and sneakers.

About three years later, I thought I made a smart move by going up the street to the projects just up the street from Crystal Avenue that we all referred to as "Da Hill." I had heard that if I really wanted to make more money, that I had to go there. It was a lot more open than the cramped hallways in C Building. Besides, someone had just gotten shot and killed in the C Building hallway and I wanted no part of that so I started hanging out with a new crew of friends. Now these guys were the real deal. Down at Crystal Avenue all we did was drink, smoke weed and sell drugs. These kids on "Da Hill" though, they were on a whole other level. All they did was sell drugs, wear the same black Champion hoody every day and pull out guns at whoever wasn't welcome there. They didn't care about appearance. Right away, I felt that I had made the biggest mistake of my life. But, one thing I knew about the drug game was that stories got around quickly, and I did not want to be known as a punk by anybody. I had made the decision to be out on the streets, so I felt I needed to go all out no matter what it took.

Then, in a blink of an eye, the next thing I knew, I was being handed a loaded gun to go and kill somebody. It was my first time ever seeing or even holding a gun. My brain just froze but I felt I had no choice than to grab the gun and follow the crew. I had to go along with the situation because these were the people who were now taking care of me financially. Aside from that, I felt I had to prove myself if "being down" was what I was trying to do. Things got "real" really quick. The crazy thing is that I hadn't even been hanging out with this new crew for longer than a month. I was a young teenager and there I was, already risking going to prison for the rest of my life. But, without hesitation, I grabbed the gun and followed orders. I felt like I was left no other choice.

We were each handed a gun like it was a toy. In fact, while on our way to searching for the guys that we were after, the leader of the crew that I had been selling for had two fully loaded guns on him. Clearly, they had done this many times before. As for me, the gun that I was handed felt like it weighed a hundred pounds. I didn't even know if I was going to be able to shoot the gun if we caught up to the kids that "they" wanted to kill. I say "they" because I had never shot a gun before, never mind ever wanted to kill anyone. But, I knew that if we caught up to them that I would have had to shoot that gun without showing them that I was afraid or scared to do so. We searched everywhere that we could for them, but thankfully, we never found them. If it meant anything at all, it at least proved to them that I was "down." What they didn't know was that I was scared shitless. Till this day, I look back and wonder where I would be right now had we caught up to those kids.

Most people usually thank God when they make it out alive from crazy situations. But, I'm going to talk to you about the Devil for a minute. I have to give him some of the credit too. If it weren't for him, I wouldn't have gone through all the things that you'll be reading about. I know some of you are thinking that I am crazy for saying that but let me explain. You see, the Devil is the best person to turn to if you want anything right away, which at that time, it's really what I felt I needed. The Devil makes it easy for us to turn to him when we want those quick benefits. As we all know, the opposite of that is God's plan because we know that he works much slower than the Devil. With God, you have to earn it before he blesses you with anything. The Devil, well … you make the request and he just pretty much hands it to you. You don't have to wish, pray or even hope for anything. It's all right there in front of you to make or take. Just like it was right there in plain view out of my 3rd floor apartment window. But, the one thing that I had to learn the hard way was that once you turn your back on the Devil and want to do better for yourself, trust and believe that he will take it all back just as fast as he gave it to you. 20 years later, I still feel like he is haunting me for turning my back on him.

For those of you that can't seem to wrap your head around understanding why people choose to deal drugs, the answer is very simple. It's really all about the easy money. Everything and anything that happens outside of that is just entirely ignorant, unpredictable and unfortunate. Although from the outside looking in, we all looked like criminals, not all of us were bad people. Yes, we made stupid choices and decisions but not everyone was out to kill each other. I am not and will never make any excuses for anyone's criminal behavior, but it wasn't like we just woke up one day and decided that we wanted to kill or be killed. All I am trying to say is that behind the scenes, most of us were really good people. It may sound weird to you, but most of those positive things that you hear people say at funerals about those that ran the streets and were murdered are somewhat true. There was always a positive side of a drug dealer or a criminal that no one ever got to see or know about. Somebody out there loved them. But, to the rest of the world who doesn't know about or understand the street life, we were all living and acting like animals.

So yes, it's really all about the easy money. Unfortunately, when you have a bunch of men too close to each other, drinking liquor, smoking weed and carrying guns with a rep to protect, there will always be those who are going to try and prove to be the biggest and the baddest of all. And that's just how people got killed or ended up in prison for life. Many dealers just took it a lot further than they should have. The reasons people killed were so stupid that even the murderer regretted it almost immediately once they were locked up. It's no different than a professional sport. There will always be that dirty player who barely ever plays by the rules. The crazy part about the drug game though is that it is usually the "he say, she say" sort of thing that will usually get you shot or killed. Especially if it has to do with a woman. I probably know of two incidents in over twenty years that involved drug dealers shooting at each other over money. Everything else was usually over gossip or some type of situation that could have either been handled by simply ignoring it or fist fighting it out. But, from my own experience and seeing just how quickly these situations occurred, if you had one on you, the gun was more than likely going to be used.

After being stuck on the streets for so many years, I didn't really have any experience at doing anything else other than selling drugs and acting stupid. Other than being a baseball player, writing is the only thing that has helped me stay sane and maybe even alive. Although I have been through a lot, I honestly can now say that I have no regrets. I have accepted everything that has happened in my life as an experience that has helped me become the man that I am today. With that being said, I've waited a long time for this moment to finally be able to share this story with the rest of the world. Sharing my story with all of you is truly a gift from God. He definitely made it possible for me to survive all that I have been through in order to be able to write these stories that may one day save your own kid's life. I hope that I can reach them before the wrong people do. Here's my story.

NEW LONDON

I've come a long way in my life. Not far enough to say that I am fully satisfied with where I am at today, but happy enough to still be here and continuing to strive to do better. I've learned many things from many different people. I've been through more than enough to understand that things in life should not be taken for granted, but that everything happens for a reason. Some of us learn faster than others to accept those situations that help mold us into the people we become, while others will just simply go all out until the very end. It's not so much that I was lost in the street world physically, but rather that I was lost in my own path mentally due to having gone through what the average person may never have had to encounter in their lives. The streets weren't the problem. It was when I felt alone that I suffered the most. That's usually when I got in the most trouble. Boredom is probably the number one reason why most of us did the stupid things that we did only to regret them seconds later. Somehow, on the road to trying to get back on track, it was really the simple conversations with those who were happy and enjoying their lives on the daily basis that allowed me to come back to reality and remember that at one point, I too, had somewhat of a good life prior to choosing the wrong path.

Just to share a little of what I mean when I say that I have been through more than what the average person would likely have encountered, I will write about situations that I personally dealt with throughout this book. But, before I get into all of that, I want you to please understand that I will never go into every detail about these drama-filled events that I personally witnessed out of respect for those who are no longer with us and the grieving family and friends who may still be dealing with their loss. I've hung out with some of the craziest and most violent people who didn't care about risking their freedom or hesitate to empty an entire clip in broad daylight. On the flipside though, I've also hung out with many who just weren't built for the streets and were quick to point their once used trigger finger to tell on others right from the witness stand.

Between all of that, I quickly learned three important rules that I always followed in order to make it out on the streets alive.

1- I never heard anything.

2- I never saw anything.

3- I most definitely never said anything.

I followed these rules not just to the cops, but also while talking with friends. Which in my opinion, that's the number one reason why most people always seemed to get caught in the end. If you did anything and bragged about it, you better believe that it would eventually be repeated. All it took was a little weed and liquor in someone's system and somehow, all your business ended up with the police. Especially if you pillow talked to women who were going back and forth between numerous men. By the time you were placed in handcuffs, you would have no idea who it was that told on you. So, not only could we not trust anyone fully with our secrets, we most definitely couldn't trust them with our lives. But, no matter how hard times got, all I ever needed to do was give myself a certain amount of time to deal, cope with and grieve if I had to and then move on from everything as quickly as possible. I always reminded myself that no matter what occurred out on the streets, that it was all just part of a game that we all had chosen to be a part of. At the end of the day, everything and anything that you had to deal with was your own choice and you played at your own risk.

Throughout all my dealings growing up, I have personally witnessed many of those things that you see on the news or read about in newspapers. I must admit, it has made me feel somewhat lucky to see firsthand the consequences that I personally had to dodge all my life, yet mentally could never escape. As to some of those situations that I have witnessed, they range anywhere from murders, to robberies, all the way down to watching people I grew up with become snitches and drug addicts. I was always trying to figure out why something that looked so simple from a distance became so crazy and violent as you got closer and deeper into it. I guess the only way that I could describe it is to compare it to those crazy people who go out into the jungle or into the deep sea to get as close as they can to the deadliest and most violent creatures out there in the wild. I couldn't understand why many of those project hallways or dead-end streets quickly turned from a party-like environment and right into a crime scene all because the wrong word was said or a simple stare took too long between blinks.

Again, out of respect for those that I have seen fall with my own eyes, I have chosen to only share an overall mental picture of the things I've seen personally. I would rather only bring you close enough to describe how certain situations can end up tragically than to put into words what a victim had to go through as they fought for their last breath. I can honestly say that from my days of living at the Crystal Avenue projects and on Belden Street in New London, CT back in the early 80s and up to the mid 90s that there was no possible way for me to escape anything negative or illegal no matter what shortcuts I took to try and avoid any of it. No matter what I tried, there was no way of dodging a drug deal going down, a needle full of heroin being shot through an addict's puffed out vein, a crack pipe being lit, a door being kicked in by a police task force, people having sex on elevators, fire alarms being pulled to muffle the sounds of gunshots, or drug dealers being robbed and literally being stripped butt naked of all their belongings. And to think, I was a witness to most of this before graduating from high school.

Being a part of such a dark and crazy world made me feel like I would never be able to recover from my past. I never thought that I would have been able to just get back to living a normal and positive life after all that I had dealt with. It wasn't simple though. Trust and love were the two things we all tried to avoid having to deal with. Being that we were all fighting over the same things and were willing to do anything to get them regardless of what it took, we only showed temporary respect towards each other until someone crossed the line and became disrespectful in any way. It was never

31

because we trusted or loved one another. At any given moment, for whatever reason, any of us could have easily become either a suspect or a victim simply because we just couldn't agree or see eye to eye on a simple matter. Most of the crimes that I was ever a part of or had witnessed were never planned. They were mostly on-the-spot decisions that left everyone shocked and speechless. Growing up in the projects surrounded by some of the most dangerous criminals and biggest drug dealers was never easy. At any time, the person you laughed with yesterday could turn into being your worst enemy and kill you the next day just because he felt you deserved it somehow. Showing fear or expressing your real emotions would have only made most feel like you were too weak to be trusted or couldn't be depended on if a situation suddenly occurred and they needed your back.

Although I was only a small dot under the microscope of the street problems and issues that you hear about, to me, street life was my everything. The only time you would have ever heard me using the word love was when it came to describing how I felt about being out there and caught up in all the bullshit. In return, this gave me all the information that I needed to share some of these experiences with you. And, even though I would love to write about the actual experiences, I would rather write about how it affected me personally and what it has turned me into today. I have never felt the need to glamourize something so negative just to amuse those who would only view it as a story to share while I was stuck dealing with it through some type of pain. Instead of just sitting around talking about those situations, I choose to use them as examples for all the parents who need to do their best to keep their children out of harm's way. I never saw the dangers of living the street life until I decided to change for the better and saw just how much more I appreciated my freedom and the ability to walk down the street without having to owe anyone or fear anything.

Unfortunately, because of my past, it has become very difficult for me to show any normal emotions or reactions like the average person should when something negative or tragic occurs. I have become desensitized to most of the things people usually find sad or emotional. Most of the situations we dealt with became conversations rather than grieving moments. It takes a lot for me to be able to express my feelings through words, let alone show emotions through tears. Compared to how I was and who I have become, I now have more time to take in most of my situations and deal with them a lot better than I used to. Back when I was younger, there wasn't enough time to dwell on things we couldn't change or do anything about. It's sad, but in most cases, some poured liquor, some smoked a blunt, and some just went and got a tattoo in memory of the ones they lost. Once they sobered up and the ink dried, it was right back to doing what they knew best.

I had to free myself from that and believe that I should no longer be living in fear and begin to give my best to any positive opportunities that presented themselves and see how far they would take me. I was willing to accept any positive chance and opportunity I came across to avoid going backwards in my life. I knew that it wasn't going to be easy and that it would require me to be more patient with the outcomes no matter how many times I tried and failed. I figured that since there was nothing worse than what I had already put myself through in the past, that taking positive chances was a lot safer than to continue taking dangerous risks. Looking back, many of the choices that I was making could have gotten me a life sentence at any time. One of the days that I always turn back to in my thoughts is when I was handed that gun at the age of 15. Till this day, that had to be one of those days that I couldn't have thanked God enough for it ending the way that it did. I'll elaborate a little more about this situation later in this book.

I am going to try to reflect and go back in time to show you some of the ways that I used to deal with my situations. I will take all that I went through and use it to give my own personal advice to some of you who may still be dealing with similar things. Please keep in mind that I have only recently found happiness. And bear with me as I try to show you how I have come to this point in my life. In this book, you will see me go back and forth with my thoughts and how I may still deal with certain situations because of how the street life affected me. I had to find a way to let go of the street way of dealing with things versus how we should deal with personal matters at home. My goal is to get you to understand that dealing with a drug dealer can sometimes be no different than dealing with a soldier that had been through a war. I want to lead you all the way to how I concluded that I not only knew that I needed to make changes in my life, but also explain how difficult it was for me to let it all go.

ROLE MODELS

Have you ever heard drug dealers say, "I didn't choose the game, the game chose me"? Or, have you ever heard them say that drugs and guns are being brought here to America for minorities to be suppressed or to kill each other? Growing up in the projects, that's all you ever heard. I can honestly say that I felt that way myself. Now that I am older and wiser, I believe that to be the excuse and the reason for us as drug dealers to use every time the argument came up about who's at fault for all the violence that's being committed out there on the streets. In order for you to understand why we as drug dealers blame and point the finger at the system is because it only seems like minorities are the ones being targeted and filling up the prisons across the country. So, let's be honest. I know that many minorities that I grew up with may disagree with me, but it all comes down to a choice. Yes, it's hard for minorities to find jobs and yes, it is very hard to be able to afford to live in better places, but at the end of the day, it is still a choice for any individual to sell drugs or to commit crimes. No one comes up to you and hires you to do it. No one puts a gun to your head and forces you to sell drugs. It may be true that we're not the ones picking up the cocaine in Colombia, but we were definitely the ones picking it up at the "re-up" spots in New York City.

In my opinion, politicians stand no chance in their efforts to clean up the streets. In fact, we shouldn't really rely on them to do so. I don't care how many police officers they put out there to patrol, drugs will always continue to be sold and guns will continue to be used. There is nothing that a politician can do except talk about it in a speech in the hopes that they get elected and then forget about it once they are in office. I honestly believe that rappers have more power in controlling drug dealers out on the streets than politicians do. Rappers cannot only relate to the problems of the streets, they can get the attention of any minority instantly with any song that they put out. Unfortunately, they, too, have a reputation to protect and must be cautious of how "soft" they may come across. It wasn't like that back in the day when you had artist like KRS-1 and Rakim trying to warn the younger kids about the dangers of the streets. And although most of their songs were great and had everyone hearing them, no one really listened until NWA released the song "Fuck the Police." It was right after that song came out that my life took a turn for the worse. For me, all hell broke loose after that. Till this day, I remember my dad walking into my bedroom and me waking up to him breaking my cassette tape in half. He didn't even say a word to me about it; he just looked at me and walked out. The very next day, I went out and bought myself a Walkman and a new copy of Straight Outta Compton cassette.

The same way that rappers had to be and sound tough, drug dealers had to do the same. Drug dealers got so caught up with having to protect the reputation of their nicknames that it seemed like they forgot what their real names were until it was called in a courtroom. In fact, it wasn't until some of them were shot or killed that we finally did learn what their first and last names really were. No one liked to be called by their real names in the streets. I guess they were either trying to hide their real identity because they didn't want anyone telling on them or because it just made them seem or sound tougher. Not all of them, but if you actually did go by most of drug dealer's nicknames, you would have thought they were real rappers and murderers.

The three people that I chose to emulate were the three people that I saw getting the most respect at the time. Although there were so many, these three were my personal favorites. Till this day, I still haven't seen anybody do it like they did. All three of them combined was who I mentally became. When they say that "the streets will have you all fucked up" I used to think it was because of the drug use. To me, it was because of who I chose to follow and wanted to be like. I wanted to do everything that they did. I wanted to make money, I wanted to look good and I was ready to intimidate and fight anybody that stood in my way. This wasn't the way that my parents raised me, but I fell in love with my new lifestyle. It got me all the attention that I was no longer getting at home. And of course, they all had nicknames.

The first person that I ever met with a hustler's nickname was Richie. There was really nothing tough about it though. Till this day, I still wonder where he got the nickname from, but if I were to take a guess, I would say he probably liked the boxer Marvin Hagler. So, that's what most people started calling him, "Marvelous", Marv for short. Of course, I never called him that myself, but I always thought it was funny. When I reminisce about him, I still picture him wearing his navy blue hat that spelled his name RICH in big white letters. Besides the hat and the big ol' chain with the Mercedes Benz medallion that he always wore, it was those big ass knots of money that he kept in his pockets that I was always staring at. And although he was making so much money at that time, he was the quietest hustler I that have ever known in my life. He never bragged about anything. In fact, he barely ever spoke to anyone outside of his small circle of friends. From him, I learned the real meaning of "hush money."

Every time I hear the verses "your jeans too tight" and "my pockets are knotty" by Jay Z, I automatically think of Richie. His jeans were always fitted, but the knots of money he always had in both pockets made you think he needed to buy a bigger size pair of jeans. The last time I saw him alive, he was standing quietly all by himself in a corner of the building he grew up in, the C building. The look in his eyes were very different to me. He looked worried. Richie had these big white teeth that I was so used to seeing every time he laughed. That day though, he seemed out of it and was even wearing a black and yellow bandana, which I thought was very strange since I was always used to seeing him wearing a hat. Till this day, I live with the regret of not standing there just another five minutes longer. By the time I got in my car and across town, I heard the bad news. He had been shot and killed in the same exact spot I last saw him standing at.

The second nickname that I was constantly hearing all the time was "Babe." And if you ever thought I had a hard time calling Richie "Marvelous" you can imagine how I felt about calling another man "Babe." I remember hearing about Babe so many times that when I finally saw who he was, I couldn't figure out where he got his nickname from. Babe, of course, was Merrill Epps. He was a giant to me. He was built like an NFL football player. And if you thought Richie was quiet about his hustle, you would have never thought anything negative about Babe. He had a great personality. And with his looks, physique, and a nickname like Babe, he probably never had to say a word to get what he wanted. Every time I got a chance to sit next to him, he would always try to give me some positive advice. He would always tell me to follow my dreams of being a baseball player and to not get involved in the drug game. Little did he know, the reason why I always wanted to be around him was because he made me feel important. It made me feel like people would accept me and not try anything with me knowing that I was friends with him. That's where I learned that everything in the streets was mostly about perception. If you wanted people not to mess with you, you had to show them that you had a little protection. And at that time, he was the one that I always wanted to hang out with every chance I could.

I still remember the first time ever I saw him. He was coming out of his building, which at the time was the A building. He was wearing a "wife beater" tank top and black basketball shorts with a pair of high-top Fila's. At the time, all I knew about "Babe" was that he was the oldest brother to this other kid I knew named Todd, who was a star football player at New London High. What I remembered the most about Babe was how nonchalant he was. He was a real smooth talker. I got so caught up with how muscular he was that I barely ever saw his feet touch the ground when he walked. It was because of him that I wanted to get in shape and began lifting weights. His physique alone made people respect him. The last time I saw him was at a bar called Lucky's. After knowing him for over 15 years, it was the first and last time we ever hugged after a handshake. He spotted me and my brother in a corner and came over to talk to us.

At that time, I believe that he had been living in Hartford and although it had been a long time since I had seen him, I still looked up to him the same way that I did when I was younger. After our quick conversation, I remember him walking back towards his group of friends on the wall to our right. As Babe turned around to walk away, I noticed a man coming in through the entrance to my left wearing a blue coat. I remember staring at the man in the blue coat as he walked in and made his way around the bar and towards the group to my right where Babe was headed. Once the man in the blue coat got to where Babe headed towards, an argument quickly broke out. I'm not sure what it was about, but Babe, as I always knew him to be protective of his friends, immediately pushed the man in the blue coat all the way to where we were standing.

46

The man in the blue coat landed so close to me that till this day I feel like I could have done something to save Babe like I know he would have done for me. Once again, I was left with the regret for not keeping our conversation going just a little longer. I went home that night and just couldn't sleep. In fact, I didn't sleep well for about two weeks straight. It was at that moment that I picked up a pen and just started writing. It became my outlet, and it was the only thing that helped me get through my toughest moments after witnessing someone being shot and dying right in front of me for the first time, especially someone that I admired, loved and wanted to be like. The man in the blue coat wasn't there longer than three minutes before firing a single gunshot that has continued to replay in my thoughts as if it was just seconds ago.

People always talk about what they would do if they were ever in a life and death situation. Everyone seems to have all the superman answers as to what they would do if they ever had to deal with a dangerous moment and had to defend themselves. Let me be the one to tell you; there is nothing that you could ever do to protect yourself once a person has already made up their mind to get to you first. As much as I wish I could go back and have done things differently that night, me trying to help Babe that night would have probably also gotten me killed. It was clear to me that the man in the blue coat only went there for one thing and that was to kill somebody. His mind had already been made up before he even confronted Babe.

For a few seconds, I truly believed that Babe was going to pull through and live. Out of everything that happened that night, the thought of watching him stand back up from the floor after he had been shot led me to believe that he was going to be okay. It wasn't until I saw him fall again by the entrance when I finally began to snap out of it and ran outside. Everything felt as if it were happening in slow motion. Once I got outside, I heard more shots being fired. I didn't know which way to run. I remember feeling like the ambulance took forever to get there. Once I made it to the hospital and saw how everyone was standing around crying and hugging each other, I knew we had lost him. Babe, I will never forget you.

Then, there was DeJohn or "D" for short. He was the only one out of the three that did not live at Crystal Avenue. Till this day, I still don't know if he was related to someone there or if he was just hustling like everyone else was in the C Building. But that to me meant nothing. What I remember most was the first time I had ever heard his voice. As I waited for the elevator, which was the same elevator that I later began using to go all the way up to the eighth floor and work my way back down the stairs looking for drug stashes to steal from the electrical sockets, I saw him holding a 40 oz. wrapped in a paper bag and hearing him demanding someone to rewind the song "Don't Believe the Hype" by Public Enemy as it blasted loudly through the hallways on repeat for about an hour. DeJohn was built like the boxer Mike Tyson, maybe a bit taller. The other thing I really noticed about him was his "hard" walk. It wasn't a smooth or a slow "dap" like all the other hustlers had. It was more of a side to side and shoulder to shoulder get out of my way type of walk. I have to admit, his walk alone was bit scary to me. The first few times that I saw him he was hanging out with his brother "Pookie" and a white kid named Shane. I thought it was a bit odd seeing a white kid hanging out with them at that time because Crystal Avenue was mostly run by the blacks who usually sold crack and weed in the C Building and by the older Puerto Ricans in the B Building where I lived where they sold cocaine and heroin.

DeJohn was very unique in a sense. One minute you would see him in a hoodie and sneakers looking like a hustler and the next he would come around the corner with a little gel in his box type haircut wearing a bright silk button-up shirt. Like Babe, he too demanded respect. He was very intimidating. And if he didn't know you, he would just give you a quick stare that would make you stop looking his way. Because I barely ever had the opportunity of really speaking to him personally, the only memories I have of him were the

50

crazy stories that others would talk about and seeing how people always crowded around him when he came down to Crystal Avenue. Every time I saw him in the projects it almost felt like there was a party going on outside. He was like a real-life movie star. From my window, I would study his every move the best I could. With his rep, I learned that you had to put a little fear in others so they would keep their distance and stay out of your business.

After so many years of going in and out of prison, DeJohn had joined the Nation of Islam. I have to admit, it was very strange seeing him on the corner selling The Final Call, but I was very proud of him. It appeared that he had finally found peace in his life and had even gotten married to a woman named Rhonda. I remember stopping by a few times to buy copies from him just to show him my support. It was one of the few times that I had actually gotten that close to him and had quick conversations with him. Although he wore nice suits as he stood out there, you could still see one battle scar in particular after having been sliced by someone on his face with a razor a few years prior. After seeing him out there a couple of times, I thought he had moved to another location because he was no longer standing on the corner of Jefferson and Garfield.

The next time I saw DeJohn was back down on Crystal Avenue. Only this time, he was not wearing a suit. An argument had broken out between a few kids that I was hanging out with. Right when they were about to fight, I was surprised to see DeJohn come out of nowhere to break them up. In his deep voice, I can still hear him saying "break it up, y'all, don't need to be out here fighting." Till this day, I didn't know what I was shocked about or impressed by the most. The fact that he was hanging out at Crystal Avenue again or just how quickly everyone listened to him and went about their way. A few days later, I saw him driving around town in a navy blue BMW 740. I remember seeing him driving up Belden Street and waving to him as he beeped his horn and quickly waived back. It was the last time I saw DeJohn alive.

Years later, after connecting and speaking to his wife Rhonda, she explained to me that she was on the phone talking to DeJohn the day that he was murdered. Rhonda mentioned that she was trying to get him to come home because she was pregnant at the time with his child and wanted him to come be with her. She said that the last words she remembers him saying over the phone were, "I know, I know, I know" right before he was confronted and shot several times by two teenage kids. I was actually headed to the same projects where he was shot because that's where one of my brothers, who was on the run at the time on attempted murder charges, had been hiding out at for several months. I remember looking out the window and watching as the police officers were walking around collecting evidence. I have to admit, I never thought anyone would have ever been that bold to approach him like that. Especially anyone that young and with a gun.

Almost everything that I did growing up as a teenager was learned from watching these men. I picked up a little from all three of them. I was young and I wanted to be just like them. I wanted to walk, talk and make money the same way that they did. I didn't realize it until I was older just how much damage I was doing to myself wanting to be like anyone else. I was lost both mentally and physically because the things that I was doing and the things that I was saying didn't feel like they were coming from me. My parents tried to raise me differently. They tried their hardest to keep us out of trouble. But, like I mentioned before, between living at Crystal Avenue and Belden Street, it was almost impossible to dodge the street game. Although most drug dealers and criminals won't admit that they were followers, it was obvious to me that in one way or another, they all learned and picked up a little from everyone that they looked up to.

If you have already read either one of my books Loser or Lie'f, you already know that I had it rough growing up. I battled and dodged many situations that others couldn't escape from. But, although I was blessed with not having to suffer as much physically like many of my friends did, I was cursed to have to live through it all mentally. I always thought that it was about luck, but the more I keep hearing that God has always been by my side, the more I started to believe it. My main goal for the near future is to slowly begin to move on from the past that I have allowed to haunt me for so many years. I have to start letting go of all of the bad and negative memories so that I can finally begin to live in peace. I have been holding onto so much that has affected me for so many years that I was always afraid to talk to someone about it because I never thought that they would understand. Everyone always seemed to have the easy answers like, let it go or leave the past in the past. Sometimes I wish it were that easy. I am going to begin by trying to accept that God above all of us knows best. It's all we can do when we find ourselves in situations we can't change.

I look back to the days before I chose to sell drugs and hung out with those that were considered to be the "wrong people" and wonder what was behind door number two? I went from being such a great kid to wanting to have the same freedoms as those I saw out of my window. I didn't fully understand it all before I made the choice to go down the wrong path. The three "role models" that I chose to admire and wanted to be like were all shot and killed before the age of 25. Since then, so many that I grew up with have been murdered, overdosed on drugs or have served many years in prison. Unfortunately, those are the trophies and retirement plan that the streets have for you in the end. I will never talk trash or feel like I am better than anyone that chooses the street life because I understand why people make that easy choice. But I will say this, no matter how many times you tell the story, the turtle will always beat the rabbit. The longer you stay out on the streets, the greater the risk will be of losing your life or your freedom.

I've learned that the key to my happiness was no longer about trying to remain relevant. It was about trying to find ways to ignore and avoid irrelevant things that have nothing to do with me. Aside from making money and being drunk or high, the street life was mostly about protecting "your boys." Everyone's loyalty just wasn't the same. Gangs, clicks, and crews were all fun at one point in my life but I also had to learn that the finger that could have been used to pull a trigger could have also been the same finger that would be used to point and snitch with. Over the years, I have realized that the streets didn't do anything other than create wars and separation between people that were at one point or another close friends, classmates or even related. In the end, crime, colors and codes seemed to be more important than life itself.

There are many situations in this world that we will always question. Part of coping with the unbelievable and unpredictable things that happen in our lives is coming to terms with understanding that we will never fully be able to accept them for what they are. Little things like laugh now, cry later. What goes around, comes around. Treat others how you want to be treated. Don't do to others what you wouldn't want done to you. What you don't know, won't hurt you. Only the good die young. Don't bite the hand that feeds you. Never burn bridges. You get the point, right? All of these sayings are just some of the examples that will come with many tears and consequences down the road when karma comes back to haunt you for all the negative things you've ever done. Because believe me when I tell you, shit does happen to all of us no matter how much we try to prevent it. But things can always get worse when it continues to come back around until you finally learn to do what's right. The bottom line is this, no matter how good you may have it in life, that day may come when you're going to need somebody to be by your side.

The fact that we have to rely on other people's sanity and state of mind should be a constant reminder to you that anything can happen at any given time in life. You don't have to read a book or watch the news to know that you can or will end up dead or in prison when you choose the street life. Those two are the most obvious. I was very lucky to dodge both. And although I still struggle sometimes, I also understand that I first have to keep looking and moving forward in life. Most of us, as minorities, are temporary and opportunistic individuals. We are so used to not having anything that we sometimes ruin great things because we abuse it to the point where it becomes nothing. We usually end up worse than before we had it.

NO ONE CARED

I come from a place where handshakes and smiles confused you into really believing that you were truly accepted and loved. A place where growing up together or being related mattered nothing over money, women, and reputation. A place where loyalty and trust usually ended once they felt they could no longer benefit from you. A place where one second ago you were breathing and the next you were being buried and forgotten about as if you never even existed. It's like watching your favorite movie over and over again, yet the ending never changed. It was a cycle of events throughout the criminal world that are really no different from the Crystal Avenue projects where I was raised all the way through the streets of Brooklyn, Chicago and all the way into the dark alleys of South Central L.A. Most disputes are similar, just a new body being locked up in a cell or buried young. Crime is crime and death is death.

No one cared if she's "your girl," "baby mom" or wife. Any time that you're not around, you better believe someone was always trying to whisper some bullshit in her ear. No one cared about who you hung around with or about how tough you thought you were. Behind your back, someone was always talking shit about you or telling others your personal business. No one cared about how much "street cred" or money you had. There was always someone waiting for the right opportunity to rob you and maybe even kill you if you made the wrong move. And in most cases, and in all of these situations, it was barely ever your enemies plotting against you. It was mostly done by your jealous friends who either wanted what you had or wanted the attention you were getting. One of the most important things to remember is that your closest ones know most of your strengths and just about all of your weaknesses. They know your every move and what you were capable of doing. As time goes on and shit gets old, they'll eventually be the ones to betray you once they got comfortable enough to do so. Everyone I've known in the streets was mostly concerned and worried about who didn't like them or who was always talking shit. But, do the history on who has snitched on who, who has robbed who, and in most cases, who turned their backs on them when they needed them the most? I remember hearing a story once about a man crying over his friend at a funeral and hugging everyone, acting like it wasn't his fault why the other one laid dead in a coffin. Yes, it was fucked up like that sometimes.

One thing that people never seem to understand is that everything in the streets is temporary. It's like the lives of cats and dogs. Some appeared to have had nine lives while others run on the streets could have been added up like dog years. Some were luckier than others while the ones we felt deserved it the least always got it the worst. Throughout my own experience, a year in the streets was a very long time. You have no idea of how many crimes you can commit and how much money you can make in that amount of time. Every single day of the year is spent doing both. In the spare time, we just got drunk or high. So, if you take a closer look at the prison time that some people are doing right now and feel that the punishment didn't fit the crime, think about this for a minute. How much time do you think they would actually be doing had they been caught for the worse act that they committed and got away with? Because in most cases, most people who are incarcerated are usually in for possession of drugs or petty violations. Everything else from robberies and shootouts were barely ever the case unless they had been told on.

The deeper you are in the streets, the closer you usually were to the truth. The further you are, the more lies and rumors you'll hear. This is where all the bullshit lies. By the time the sun rose the next morning, you would have heard that "such and such" did it and this was why. Most of the times when I heard the stories, the suspects they named was usually never the one who ended up being charged or the victim was always being misidentified. No one barely ever really knew the truth from the gossip that was being spread. Everyone always had their own version, even if ten people saw the same exact thing. And even when the ones who really knew did talk about it, no one seemed to believe them anyway. In the end, none of it really mattered unless they were willing to go and testify to it in a courtroom, which was very rare when I was growing up. These days though, like in the game of monopoly, some have used it as their get out of jail free card.

Anyone who is out there huslin' drugs, in a gang, or committing crimes together and really thinks that they can trust everyone in their circle is an idiot. Snitching has become very easy for most. Keeping their mouths shut in the heat of the moment is very difficult, especially if they are being pressured for information while fighting for their own freedom. You'll be surprised what a few cigarettes can do for them during the first 48. There will always come a time where someone will say "fuck it" and just give up your name and everything that you have ever done without even knowing you personally. But why be confused about it?

In all reality, you only came across the people you hang out with because you chose to sell drugs and commit crimes together. Not because it was meant for you to be the best of friends. It was always easy to commit crimes together. But it was always hard for many to "keep it real" once they ended up in handcuffs. One of the street's codes has always been that a self-proclaimed thug should never crack under pressure according to those out on the streets, no matter the situation. But that for sure wasn't always the case.

The same thing that most people did the very next day after a wedding was usually the same exact thing that they did the very next day after a sentencing or a funeral. Sober up and carried on. They'll talk about it for a few days until something worse or more entertaining occurred. I have to admit, I myself didn't care about most if not all of the people I came across outside of our circle. None us really did. Unless you were dealing with or for us, you were just a handshake and maybe a quick conversation that carried no weight. There was no trust, no loyalty, and definitely no love. In most cases, it was usually someone who wasn't a part of the crew that brought all of the problems to our neighborhood and even to our front door. No one was safe. At any given time, you could have lost everything you ever made or had.

In the end, no one cared about how cool or about how young you were. No one cared about how many kids you left behind or that a mother would be left crying for years over their son. No one cared about whether you served one year in prison or twenty-five to life. In fact, in the end, all they really cared about was that they were not the ones suffering in any way. Every man was for himself when the cops came or when the bullets rang out. You had to be cautious and alert every day to avoid both. You couldn't really look back until you were in a safe place. Unfortunately, everyone usually ran the same way while becoming easier targets to catch or be killed. And once the smoke cleared and the dust settled, a little liquor here and a few blunts later, things went back to normal within a few days like nothing ever happened.

RUN OR BE RAN

Let's rewind back a bit to the year 1986. I was about 11 years old and had been living in the projects now for about 2 years. Everything and everyone seemed to be so peaceful. Well, except for those days where we used to get roughed up a bit by those who would corner us because they always thought we were talking about them when we spoke that "mira, mira go back to Puerto Rico shit." The black kids never liked it when we spoke Spanish around them. I wasn't sure if it was just their excuse for wanting to beat us up or because they actually thought we were talking about them. Either way, it forced us to have to learn how to speak English the hard way. But aside from that, all of us would always get together and either play a pick-up game of basketball, baseball, or football on the concrete between the buildings of the Crystal Avenue projects. I never really understood why, but my dad was always warning us about staying right in front where he could see us.

At home, we would always play Monopoly, Checkers or Uno. It was what kept us all together and having fun as a family. There wasn't a day that I didn't look forward to playing those games. We were all so competitive that we would sometimes stay up all night arguing and trying to beat each other, especially when we played Monopoly. I always wanted to win all the money and end up with all the properties. Crack had already slowly begun to make its way right into our projects. Who would have known that the game of Monopoly sort of became a game that we all began to play in real life? Those dice became so addictive that they were taken off the board game and right into the hallways where we were all trying to get real money instead.

We wanted it all. We wanted the cars and houses that we saw on tv. We wanted the money and the beautiful women that we saw on shows. We even wanted to be tough and crazy just like the actors or rappers we saw in movies and videos. If an actor or musician wore something that looked nice or was in style, you could easily tell who was making money in the projects because they too would also be wearing the same name brand of clothing. Especially if hip-hop artists were wearing it in their videos. To be honest, at times, I couldn't really tell the difference between what I was seeing on television from what was actually happening right there in front of us all. You didn't have to be a genius to know who was dealing drugs from who was using it either.

All it took was for you to see the hand to hand exchange and then the addicts walking away quickly to go shoot up, snort, or smoke what they had just bought. About an hour later, you would see them coming right back to buy more because the high from smoking crack didn't last very long. Years later, most of those crack addicts switched over to using heroin because they believed that the high lasted longer, and it was much cheaper to buy. The drug game moved pretty fast, but it didn't take long before I began to understand the street life. It all started there at the Crystal Avenue projects in New London. From one day to the next, we went from asking for a few quarters to buy candy to filling our pockets with hundreds of dollars to buy new sneakers and clothes.

Here's how it all began. By this time, I was 12 years old and in the 8th grade. I remember looking out of the window one day and noticing how the crowds of people that used to hang outside quadrupled out of nowhere. It became much rowdier, yet more exciting in a sense. The music got louder and louder, and the smell of piss and marijuana pretty much just took over the hallways. I remember how tuned in I became to all the action that was taking place right in front of my building. Although I was very young, it was obvious to me that the people who were just standing around were the "bad guys" and the dirty looking people who were coming around were the addicts. The interactions between the two usually only lasted for about 10 seconds. Anything longer than that was a problem. Drug dealers didn't talk much. Drugs in one hand and a joint or beer in the other. So, when an addict came to buy the drugs, they had to already have the right amount of money in hand. And if they were short with the money, there was a great chance that they would have gotten beat up right out of their shoes and robbed of their money. They became sort of like punching bags for anyone who wanted to test their strength. I can't tell you how many times I have seen addicts literally get laid out from one punch all because someone made a bet just to see who would knock them out first. Crazy thing was that a few hours later, with their eyes blackened and shut, they would just come right back to the same person that punched them and buy drugs from them.

All of these things that I was witnessing were things that I obviously was not supposed to be seeing or raised to be like. The most violence we were ever allowed to see was when we were watching WWF on television. But, living in the projects, there was really no telling what we were going to see or hear next. There were three buildings in our projects. We lived on the 3rd floor of the B Building. Building C being the worse one of the three was directly right outside of our kitchen window. I could see everything from there. Once we were told that we had to come in the house from playing outside, I would take a shower and rush straight to the window to be nosy. I'm not sure why my parents never said anything about it, but I was really up to no good. I became fascinated with watching the dealers and how they moved, the way they dressed, the way they talked, and even with the way they walked. As a twelve-year-old, I have to admit, I was impressed with almost everything that they did. I started to pick up on who was who and who did what, all from that third-floor window.

One day, while sitting there, I noticed that the cops were heading straight to our projects. From my window, I could literally see the police department from a distance and was able to tell whenever they were going to rush into the projects and try to arrest the dealers. I couldn't really be too obvious because I didn't want my parents to hear me, but I made a quick sound and pointed over towards the street to warn the dealers that the cops were coming. They picked up on what I was trying to tell them, and they all quickly ran into the building. Once the cops came in and left, the dealers all came back outside slowly. One of them looked up towards me in the window and said thank you for the warning. I instantly felt like I was a part of them. I felt like I did something really cool. I became a look out kid for all the drug dealers in the front plaza from that day on.

After that, every time I would go outside, most of the dealers were now shaking my hand. I felt like they were my boys. I started picking up and listening in on all of the things that the dealers said and what they did while they waited for the addicts to come. Most of the time, all they really did was drink liquor, smoke weed, play dice games, and talk shit all day. And when they weren't talking shit to or about each other, they were talking about all the women they had or wanted to sleep with. Everything that I had been taught to believe before the age of twelve began to feel more like it was all just a big ol' lie. There wasn't a single thing that they did or talked about that I wasn't interested in. Everything changed from one day to the next. I was slowly beginning to feel like I was being accepted as one of them. All it took was a few simple warnings to them out the window that the cops were on their way, and I felt like I was a part of their crew.

Now mind you, I had no idea what it was they were dealing at the time, let alone what the taste of liquor or weed was like. The closest thing that I ever knew or heard about when it came to drugs was that commercial "This is your brain, this is your brain on drugs" by Nancy Reagan and then when they announced that Len Bias had died right after being drafted from smoking crack cocaine. Other than hearing a little about drugs being bad for you at school, that was all I really knew. In fact, at that time, I had never even seen a bullet or had ever held a gun in my own hands before. I hadn't even kissed a girl yet, let alone had sex. The way these dealers talked every day, you would have thought they were in their forties with all that they had already been through. In reality, the oldest ones were about 18 while the youngest ones were about thirteen, and they had already been selling drugs since they were about ten. In fact, there was a dealer who I later sold drugs for named Eugene who had about three cars in the parking lot before the age of 16. I barely ever saw him driving though; he didn't even have a driver's license. He was the first dealer to let me borrow some of his sneakers so that I wouldn't have to be so embarrassed about the ones I always wore. In fact, his car was the first one I had ever seen with tinted windows. He never wanted to be seen driving by the cops which explained the quick trips that he would take every once in a while.

At one point, it was rare to see police cars rushing in or officers walking around patrolling our projects. I couldn't really pick up or understand why things got really crazy from one day to the next, but it was wild. Long story short, once I realized that it was a new drug they called "crack" I then understood why everyone from the dealers to the addicts were all of a sudden acting differently. In fact, right after Len Bias died and I began seeing more crack commercials on television, I began to figure out that whatever they were talking about on the news was probably exactly what was being sold right there in our projects. And one day, by accident, I found out that was the case.

While I was still debating on whether I should ask Richie for a few vials of crack to deal and start making a little money for myself, that decision was pretty much made for me. Like everything and anything that occurs in the drug world, I was introduced to the drug game almost without a choice. Although I was contemplating becoming a drug dealer and talking to Richie about it, I was always scared about getting caught or having my parents find out. To be honest, I wanted to have all the nice clothes and sneakers that they had. Above all, I wanted to be a part of something that from the outside looked cool to be "down with." I saw how being a drug dealer and having nice clothes and money made them feel confident. My situation at home was getting no better, and I was getting a lot less attention. As I write this, I feel stupid looking back at how unknowledgeable I was about adult business.

Looking back and now being a parent myself, I understand it a hell of a lot better. But things happened so fast, I almost felt like it was meant for me to sell drugs.

Like any other day, while watching others playing touch football on the concrete between the B and C buildings, I noticed about five police cars rushing into the projects. One of the dealers that was sitting closest to me quickly said, "Hold this." I couldn't put it all together at that moment, but he passed me a Coke can. I couldn't understand why he would want me to hold a soda can for him, but because it had all happened so quickly, I thought nothing of it. I placed it right there in front of me and between my legs. Up against the wall, and right in front of me were sprayed letters that read "Run or be Ran." Right next to that were about 15 to 20 drug dealers being searched. After about 30 minutes, they were all set free when nothing was found in their possession. The dealer that told me to hold onto his can came right over to me, reached in his pocket and handed me a $20 bill. You would have thought that he had handed me a million dollars by the way I felt. He asked, do you know why I'm giving you that money? I quickly responded by saying "no." He said, "Twist open the top of the can and you'll see why." So, I twisted the top off and immediately saw a plastic sandwich bag full of what looked like chunks of off-white colored chalk. He then said, "You saved me from getting arrested; that's crack inside of that can." From what he had just said and what I had been hearing on the news, I quickly figured out that I was just holding onto one of the most powerful drugs that have ever hit the streets.

After that, I wanted to hold his drugs every day. I could make $100 a week just for holding the can right next to me; so, I did. Once I figured out how much a single rock of crack cocaine went for, I just started selling it for him. Now, every time he came looking for his can I was actually handing him some money too. Because I was young and had no idea about the rules of the drug dealing game, I was being given $30 for every hundred that I made. It doesn't seem like a lot now, but for a twelve-year-old kid it was more than enough. I was making money as a dealer, and I was also making extra money on the side because I was stashing some of their drugs in our apartment. Of course, my parents never had any idea. I was even tossing it out of the window for them every time they ran out from selling all that they had. I thought I was a pro. The rush of it all felt so good that I forgot all about the consequences if I had ever gotten caught. I think I paid more attention to my parents not catching me than I did to the cops who were watching.

One thing led to another and before I knew it, I was hanging out in those hallways with some of the biggest drug dealers my hometown had ever seen or heard of. The rules inside the building were very different from what was going on out in the front plaza. In the hallways it was all about taking turns. It was the first time I ever heard the words, you cut my throat, which simply meant that you had taken someone else's turn to make their money. I lost count of how many times I saw people arguing and fighting over that. I thought that it was even crazier to see some of them pulling out a gun on an addict that they had never seen before and forcing them to smoke the crack right there in the hallway just to prove that they weren't an undercover cop. I quickly learned that the hallways just weren't for me. There was just way too much going on, and I couldn't really keep up. I started to fear the dealers more than I did the cops.

I soon learned that Run or be Ran pretty much meant that if you weren't from Crystal Avenue, you simply just weren't welcome. And if you weren't fast enough to make it across the street before getting caught, there was a good chance that something really bad was going to happen to you. Anything from getting jumped, stabbed or worse, probably could have gotten you killed. It got so bad that whenever you ordered Chinese food or Domino's Pizza, you had to go pick it up across the street because they too were afraid of having to walk through the hallways at night. It was all fun back then, but looking back, I don't know what most of us were thinking. I'm not sure if it was luck or meant to be, but I don't know how most of us even made it out alive from Crystal Avenue.

Crack ruined many people's lives. I saw some of the most beautiful women go from having pretty smiles to having ashy lips and missing most of their front teeth. It even turned the normal weed and cocaine dealers from being average money makers to wanting to be killers overnight. They said that all it would take was just one hit of crack and you would be automatically hooked on it forever; there was no turning back from that. So, between the dealers wanting to make more money and the addicts coming around nonstop throughout the day and night, it was no wonder why people were trying to kill each other over it. After a while, it seemed as if though it was no longer about the money anymore. It became all about power and respect, and that sure as hell wasn't my reason for wanting to sell drugs. All I wanted was new sneakers and nice clothes; that was all.

Once I decided to get away from the hallways and started hanging out in other projects and on different street corners, I felt a little more comfortable. I went from the overcrowded hallways of Crystal Avenue to sitting on the electrical transformers on "Da Hill" of Federal Projects and onto then meeting some of the "grimiest" hustlers on the corners of West Coit and Belden Street, where we later moved to in 1992. The streets were a lot more fun, but they were also a lot more dangerous. At Crystal Avenue, anyone that came through had to be from there or had to be cool with someone that would be okay with them hanging out. Out on the street corners though, you just couldn't control that all the time. I quickly became aware of my surroundings and had more room to run and hide from the cops or any other type of danger that came my way. We didn't care about who's property or yard we had to go through to get away when things happened. But, one thing was for sure, you had to own a gun to be a hustler on those corners. Crystal Avenue was like playing cops and robbers. West Coit and Belden was more like dealing with chain snatchers and stickup kids. Dealers didn't even care who they were selling their crack to. It was sad that even some of my own friend's parents used to come around trying to buy drugs from us. And no matter how many times I would turn them away, they would just keep coming back. It's crazy how just trying to make a few dollars created so many problems for everybody. Overall, we actually lost more than we ever gained. It's very true when they say "money comes and money goes." Unfortunately, so did the people.

I have to admit that being a drug dealer at Crystal Avenue back in the eighties and early nineties was the easiest money anyone could have ever made without having to work hard for it. You could have easily made a thousand dollars on a good day without ever having to stand up from the project benches like Richie always did. Making money was easy, yet everything else around it could have easily cost you your life if you weren't paying close attention. You just never really knew what was going to happen out of the blue. One-minute hustlers would be sitting there telling stories and the next you would have been reading about them in the newspapers the very next day. But, just like the addicts were addicted to the drugs, we were just as addicted to the money.

RAZOR

Most of the crazy drug dealers and murderers that people will ever really get to know about are the ones that they see in the movies. People's fascination with thugs, drugs, and violence is nothing new. Whether they admit it or not, most people are curious about it. You don't even have to be from the streets to be somewhat interested or attracted to it. Examples of that would be watching people like Tony Montana in Scarface, Nino Brown in New Jack City, O'Dog in Menace to Society, or even Nas and DMX in the movie Belly. As for me, I've actually hung around some of the craziest drug dealers that came really close to being just like those actors. It's hard to believe that there are some that are worse than the roles that those actors played in those films but believe me, they are out there. Knowing what I know and seeing what I have seen, the ideas for those movies are not just thoughts. I feel like I have lived some of those movies in real life.

Out of all the people that I've ever hung out with, there was this one guy in particular that for some reason, I admired the way he handled things out there in the streets. This guy was the real deal all the way around. Although I had learned a lot from Richie, Babe and DeJohn, there was this kid known as Razor. He was one of the craziest hustlers I ever hung out with. I used to hear people talk about him and say that he wasn't as real as I'm saying he was, but I never saw any of those people testing him either. This dude was probably top three of the craziest people I've ever known. Aside from my brother P and DeJohn, I didn't know anyone else that was crazier out there in the streets. He cared nothing about anyone or anything except his money, his crew, and his street rep. In fact, I'm not even going to lie, I did everything I was supposed to do around him just so he wouldn't feel like I was crossing him in any negative way. When I made the money from the drugs he supplied me with, I would make sure to pay him first before I started to work on my own profit. Out of respect, I never wanted him to ever have to come and ask for it.

I hung out with many different types of dealers in the streets, but Razor was the first street hustler and thug that I really got a chance to hang out with on a daily basis and get to really know. He probably never knew this, but he's the one that I learned the most from on how to protect myself. I met him out on "Da Hill" when I decided that I didn't want to risk selling drugs in the hallways of Crystal Avenue anymore. I met him when I was around 15 years old. He wasn't that much older than I was, but the way he carried himself and with that gun, you would have thought he had been out on the streets since he was five years old. He was about my height but with a fully grown beard. What made him look even crazier were the dark sunglasses and his mouth full of gold teeth with his hat always turned to the side. For some reason and I can't explain why, his personality always reminded me of the rapper Redman.

By the time I met Razor, I had already been hustling for about three or four years. But from the very first time that I met him, I studied him the same way that I had studied those out of my 3rd floor window at Crystal Avenue. Razor did it all. A knife in one pocket, a stash of crack and weed in the other, a gun on his waist, and sometimes he even carried mace. But, his main thing was the razor that he carried in his mouth. He loved that razor. So much so that you thought he was chewing gum until you actually saw him shift it with his tongue from one side of his jaw to the other. He was like a walking 20-year prison bid just waiting to be sentenced. He was ready for war even on peaceful days. But instead of me just saying, "Nah, this dude is nuts," and separating myself from him, it got me to want to hang out with him even more. He was the craziest member of that crew that I was talking about earlier when we went chasing after those kids with guns. Looking back, I remember that there were some days that I would just sit there and question why out of all the people I could be hanging out with, I ended up risking my life and freedom on a daily basis next to him. There was nothing positive that was going to come out of hanging out with him. This was the kind of guy that would take a sentence from a judge with a smile on his face.

I will always remember standing next to him as he practiced spitting the razor out over and over again and watching it land in the palm of his hands, like he was just spitting out sunflower seeds. I'm not going to lie, I thought that razor was eventually going to slice his tongue in half one day. But, it seemed like he had mastered it so well that he was even doing it while he was drunk and high. It was both, the craziest and most fascinating thing I had ever seen. I had never seen anything like it at the time. It was definitely fun to watch. So much so, that I began doing it myself. And although the main reason for carrying a razor in your mouth would be to serve as protection in case you got into a fight, I always feared getting punched in my face first before even having a chance to spit it out. I never really knew if he ever did slice anyone, but because I knew that he was so fast to pull out his gun, it would have been nothing for him to "buck 50" anybody across the face if he ever had to. And one day, I, too, thought I could do the same.

I remember stepping out one summer night with a few of my friends. We were heading to a party on the other side of town. As I got closer to the house party, I noticed that there was this kid that I had been looking for because he had been talking a lot of shit about us. I reached into my pocket and grabbed the pack of razors that I had bought earlier that day. I handed one to everyone who was with me that night. I told them that I was about to run up on the kid and slice his face up for all that disrespectful stuff he was saying. I guess he thought he was tough because he was hanging out with out-of-towners at the time. To me, he was nothing but a "block hopper" who could never be trusted because he was always being seen hanging out with different drug dealers every other day. As I got closer to him, he spotted me right away and just took off running.

After that night, I would spot him around town in different cars. But then, I didn't see him hanging out again for several years. I believe he ended up doing a little time in prison. When I finally did see him again, he was hanging out on West Coit Street where all my boys were at. Of all places we could have sold drugs at, we made most of our money right there next to a church. Apparently, one of my cousins was friends with him, so I knew that somehow, someway, I was going to have to let that beef go.

As I was walking closer towards him after all those years of not seeing him, I noticed that everyone started to run and scatter all over the street. At first, I was confused. Then, I heard the loud pops, but I thought it was just fireworks since it was around July 4th weekend. I noticed that the kid that I had an issue with a few years back was running towards me as I continued hearing more and more pops, only this time I began hearing two different sounds. I quickly looked across the street and spotted a man shooting his gun and it appeared that he was now pointing it my way. I'm not sure who the man was aiming for, but those bullets were sure as hell ricocheting off the wall to my left. As the kid got closer to me, his left arm hit my chest as he ran past me. A bullet that appeared to have been heading my way hit him just above his elbow, sending his arm flying up as I saw blood begin to stream down from it. I was headed towards this kid, not knowing what the outcome was going to be like, and his arm ended up shielding a bullet that was probably going to kill me. Instead of wanting to catch up to him and settle our dispute, I instead wanted to thank him for unintentionally saving my life. Street life was weird like that sometimes.

I always had the worse luck trying to run away from shootouts. Right after I realized that the man appeared to be reloading his gun and starting shooting again from across the street, I ran through my cousin's back yard and hopped the fence. With my luck, I ran right into the person the shooter was initially trying to kill. When I saw him on the other side, he asked if I could give him a ride across town. Because of my history of regretting not being able to save my own friend's lives, I didn't want to leave him for dead and then have to live with it later. So, I went and got my car and picked him up. While we were in my car, he began apologizing for what had occurred. He told me that just minutes before the shooting he had gotten into it with another kid at a gas station. He said that there was no way of him being able to warn us about the man who began shooting from across the street because it wasn't the man that he had the altercation with at the gas station. Apparently, it was one of his boys who came to retaliate.

Those gunshots were now getting a little too close to me. The first two times something like this had happened to me was while I was hanging out on "Da Hill" a few years prior. There was this kid named J that had been going back and forth with this kid named "Tiger" from Brooklyn. I remember everyone being nervous because they thought J was hiding somewhere in the bushes and was going to jump out to try and shoot Tiger. We had been warned to keep an eye out for J because they had been saying that at any moment, he would probably come through shooting. Before you know it, from the end of the parking lot, dressed in all black with his hoodie and mask on, J comes out firing. I started running towards Crystal Avenue and when I looked back wondering why the bullets were flying my way, I noticed that Tiger was running right behind me while J just kept trying to shoot him. I want to say that it was about 8 or 9 shots that were fired from J's gun; all of them missed.

Once we made it halfway down to Crystal Avenue, Tiger says to me that "This isn't over, I'm from Brooklyn and "I'm gonna show him how we get down in Brooklyn." I knew he meant business because of the look in his eyes and by the tone of his voice. He was very upset. We shook hands and went our separate ways. I remember going to bed that night wondering if something else had happened while I slept. As soon as I walked outside, I heard about what had happened. Tiger had caught up with J earlier that next morning and shot him three times in his back. J was in the hospital for a few days but he survived the shooting. I never saw Tiger after we had shaken hands and parted ways that night. A few years later, I heard that Tiger was shot and killed in Brooklyn. After he died, I heard stories about him being a stick-up kid out there in "the city" and that it had finally caught up to him.

The second time that I almost got shot, I was standing in a Burger King parking lot while I was talking on a pay phone. Behind me, there were a bunch of kids playing basketball. As I stood there on the phone, I noticed a car drive by slowly as if they were trying to see who was there on the court. They continued driving a little further down the street and then parked the car. About five kids jumped out and began running back up the street and our way. Again, with my luck, the kid they were aiming for just happened to run across the street and towards where I was standing. As he ran past me, they just continued shooting at him. It all happened so fast that I never even thought about hanging up the phone and running to a safe place. Three of those bullets hit the playscape that was right behind me. Thankfully, there were no kids playing there that day.

I had mentioned earlier in this book that leaving the hallways of Crystal Avenue to sell drugs was one of the biggest mistakes I had ever made. Mostly everything outside of those hallways of Crystal Avenue was handled without the use of a gun. Hustlers from Crystal Avenue used to love showing off by fighting things out with their hands. It wasn't until I met Razor and his boys that I began falling in love with guns. Right around the time that I was handed that gun for the first time to go look for those kids, Razor and his crew had been out on bond on attempted murder charges for a shooting that they had been involved in just a few weeks before. This was crazy to me because, had we caught up to those kids, Lord knows how many more charges they would have ended up with. But, that was him. I didn't know if shooting a gun or slicing someone was more important to him than making money. I just loved the rush I felt when I hung out with him. I remember watching Menace to Society for the first time and listening to Kane describe O'Dog in the beginning of the movie and it reminded me of just how Razor was. To me, Razor was the Dominican version of O'Dog in real life.

Out of all of all the members of his crew, I believe that Razor was the one that was sentenced to do the most time. I didn't see Razor again until he was released about seven years later. By that time, I wasn't as deep into the streets as I was back when I was hanging out with him. When I heard that he had been released, I went to his house to visit him. The first thing I did right after I shook his hand was pay him the hundred dollars I owed him before he went in. Those seven years didn't change him in any way. He went in as Scarface and came out as Carlito Brigante. A few months after he was released, I heard a story that the cops chased him near a pond where he ended up jumping in with a loaded gun to avoid getting caught. Once the cops drove off, he ended up moving out of state and I have not seen or heard anything about him since.

2 KILOS

One of the craziest parts of the street game is just how many people become so brainwashed into committing crimes solely based on their friendship. It was always hard for me to try to understand just how loyal people were towards each other while risking their life or freedom over it. Most were into protecting each other more than they actually did for their own family members. Aside from snitches though, the hardest thing to try and ever figure out was who to be loyal to and who you could trust the most. Loyalty towards certain people would have had you in some of the most difficult situations that you could ever get involved in or out of, especially when the ones you were most loyal to lived and acted as if they had nothing to lose.

I myself had fallen for this type of situation many times. You always had to be ready without hesitation to back each other up. Everyone in the streets usually picks two kinds of people to hang around with. The ones who are making the most money and the ones who had the most guns and didn't care to use them. Basically, money and power was what everyone needed to protect themselves from their enemies. But if you had both, you were in good shape. You could have been the biggest punk out on the streets, but if others noticed who you hung around with and saw that you were making money, the chances of them trying to cause any problems with you were slim. For some reason or another, I always ran with the best of the best at making money and the worst of the worst when it came to crime. Although I wasn't in it to get rich or end up in prison or dead, those types of situations were very unpredictable.

I remember being around 16 years old when I first met this guy who was new to our Crystal Avenue projects. He seemed to be a very likeable guy. I was introduced to him by one of my best friends. Like Babe and DeJohn, this kid was also a giant in size compared to me. He stood about 6'1 and weighed about 220 pounds, all of it muscle. He was built like the Terminator. What really made me wonder about him sometimes was just how many different pairs of sneakers and outfits he had. I never saw him pulling out money or making any drug sales to make me think that he was a dealer just like us. I knew that there was something about him, I couldn't figure out just what it was. But, after a few weeks, I was able to catch my first glimpse of him taking a few hits off the blunt that my best friend at that time had just passed to him. I didn't even know he smoked, but who am I to judge; I sold drugs and carried guns myself. As the days and weeks went by, I noticed that the crowd of friends got bigger and bigger around him as he sat on the benches. Everyone seemed to like him and wanted to hang out with him, including myself.

Fast forward to about a year later, this guy was suddenly making way more money than all of us. In fact, he quickly became our supplier. What was good about him was that when I gave him my cut of the money to pick it up in New York, he actually never charged me anything extra. Whatever the price was in NY was exactly what I had to pay him for. It was crazy the way that this guy moved though. He did everything with a smile on his face that stretched all the way to both sides of the two big ass diamond earrings he had on his ears. The more I thought about it, the more I began to think that wherever he had moved from, that he was either on the run from the police or just felt like he had to set up shop somewhere else. Most of the guys that I knew who come from "the island" and went straight to pushing that much weight around were deeply connected somehow. But, we needed him around for both the money and power. As we became closer friends and partners in the game, there was still that one thing about him that I really just couldn't figure out. While most were concerned, I was just curious.

Finally, one early Saturday morning I got a phone call from him. It was the first time in my life that ever I heard the word "kilo" when referring to drugs. I knew what it was, but to my knowledge, no one in my projects ever got close to that level. The moment I heard it though, it sounded more like Lotto to me. Remember, I was just a single little petty drug dealer trying to make money for sneakers and clothes. So, the very first time that I ever heard the word kilo, it made me feel like I finally made it to the big leagues. I pictured myself spending thousands before I even saw a dollar from it. The longer we spoke, I began to get a little nervous because I didn't like to talk about drugs, guns or problems over the phone. So, I told him that I would meet him wherever he was at. He said okay and we hung up. I got dressed quick because I didn't want to miss out on the opportunity of making all the money that I was already picturing myself counting in my thoughts.

I remember leaving my apartment and walking towards the State Pier projects which were directly across the street from where we both lived. Finally, I arrived and knocked on the door. He opened, shook my hand and then offered me something to drink. As I was sitting there at the table with him and talking about this kilo that he had mentioned over the phone, I began to feel a little concerned about it. Back then and even till this day, the only things that I have ever feared was getting locked up for life, getting killed or having to kill someone. And the more we talked, the more one of those three things began to feel like they were more than likely about to occur. From one second to another, my heart began beating faster and faster from both the excitement and the fear of what was about to occur.

He tells me that he was expecting a shipment around noon. He had sent someone up to New York to pick up a kilo for him. The guy that he sent was also picking one up for himself. Finally, I was going to be able to see just who this guy was working with or working for. He mentioned that we had about an hour to spare before the guy was due to arrive. The closer we got to the time, the more nervous I became. About a half hour before the shipment arrived, he passed me a loaded gun. He says to me, "When you see him pulling up in his green car and he walks into the building, I want you to stick him up and take both kilos from him and if he

makes any noise or tries to fight back, just shoot him."
So, here I am thinking that he was going to supply me
with a kilo and then suddenly it is turning into a stickup
and maybe even a homicide. I was very confused. "Why
am I sticking up the guy who is bringing you your kilo?"
I asked. He said, "So we can get both of them." This guy
was not playing, he was dead serious. I questioned the
entire situation, but I had already made up my mind that
I needed that money. I had to go through with it because
it was too good of an opportunity for me to pass on.

So, the time comes, and I see the green car
pulling into the parking lot. I'm watching him as he
pulls out his cell phone and my guess is that he was
calling to let my "friend" know that he had arrived.
They talked for about 10 seconds and hung up. He sat
in his car for about another minute and suddenly I see
him grabbing a bag and then reaching to open the car
door. Remember, I was never told or given the name of
this person. All I knew was that the color of the car was
green and that he was bringing up two kilos. My hands
were shaking so bad that I didn't even know if I was

going to be able to go through with it. My heart was pounding harder and harder by the second. Then, suddenly, I finally got to see who his connection was through the second-floor window. My hands just stopped shaking and my heart began to slowly relax. I knew that I couldn't go through with this robbery. As a matter of fact, I was completely caught off guard by who it was. I knew this guy personally. He lived two floors up from our apartment at Crystal Avenue and was also a friend of mine. The crazy thing was that I didn't even know that he sold drugs too, especially at that level.

I stood there in that hallway staring out that window not knowing if I should have thanked God that I didn't have to rob or kill him or to be upset that I was no longer going to be able to get that kilo in my hands. I heard the door opening to my left as he slowly walked towards where I was standing. He comes up to me and shakes my hand and asked, "Are you okay?" I looked him in his eyes and responded, "Yea, I'm okay." As our hands slowly separated from the handshake, I said to him, "Be safe" as he walked away from me. He said, "Same to you" and proceeded to walk down the hall and into the apartment to drop off the package. I felt like Al Pacino did in Scarface when he didn't blow up the car bomb because the kids were in the car. It was one of the most intense situations that I have ever put myself through in my life. A few minutes later, I noticed the guy again walking past me to go about his business. I walked down the hall, knocked on my friend's door and I noticed that he answered with that same ol' smile on his face. He asked, "What happened?" I responded, "I couldn't do it, I know that guy." He just laughed about it and carried on with a conversation about something else and we just moved on.

STREET LEGEND

Selling drugs to me was like going fishing; a bag of sunflower seeds in one hand and a beer in the other while hanging out with friends. Most of it was a waiting game, but we sure knew how to have a great time. On a good day we could make anywhere between a few hundred dollars and maybe even up to a thousand. When things were slow, we just sat around picking each other's brains. Not all of us were as stupid and ignorant as everyone thought. But, one thing was for sure; we always found a way to keep from being bored. We got drunk or got high and then told stories that were mostly exaggerated just to pass the time. We rolled dice and argued over money all day. Some days it got so serious that we had to end the games before it led to someone reaching for their gun. We were all "boys" but it got a little questionable when it involved gambling our money. I remember one day when I beat one of my friends in a dice game and nearly left him broke. He was so hot and frustrated that he had to take his shoes and socks off to finish the game. We had a lot of love for each other but judging by how he began talking to me, I knew that he was taking it personally. I beat him out of about $500 that day. When the game was over, I gave him half of his money back. Not because I was afraid of him, but because I didn't want money to come between our friendship. About six months later, he was sentenced to life in prison for murder.

Those were the kinds of people I once called friends. Again, most of us were likeable guys, we just did horrible things in the heat of the moment. Only those out there on the streets understand that though. We had each other's backs like how military soldiers do during a war. No matter how much we fought and argued with each other, we all truly cared for one another regardless of how everyone else felt about us. In fact, about two months before he allegedly committed murder, I sat down and had a really long conversation with him. I remember telling him that I wanted to see him finally get out of the street game and get his life together. He was married at the time, which again, was very rare for any hustler out on the street. He even cried on my shoulder after I told him that he was too good of a person to continue doing wrong. But, he was a street legend in my hometown and in most cases, those kinds of people would rather live and die playing that role. He had been in the street game for as long as I knew him.

I barely ever saw him doing anything other than hanging out on the streets. In fact, I remember how happy he was when we took him to New Jersey for a basketball game. To us, it wasn't about the basketball game. I was trying to show him and my brother P that there was much more to life than just hanging out on a corner all day. Sometimes though, you just couldn't reach people in ways that you wanted to. A positive life sometimes just isn't meant for people, it just bores them. I'm still not sure why he liked me as much as he did, but anytime we spoke, it was never about the streets. We spoke about life and things that were going on around the world. We were so cool with each other. One day, this other kid I knew from "Da Hill" had been robbed of his gold chain. When they described the person who they said did it, I remember going straight to "my boys" house and asking him for the chain. I just knew it was him. I didn't think that he would, but I was able to somehow talk him into handing me the gold chain so I could return it to the owner.

One of my best memories of him came while we sat in my car and listened to the song "Ether" by Nas for the first time. He knew that I was a diehard Jay Z fan, so he wanted me to hear how Nas had just destroyed Jay Z on it. I had just picked him up from the mall where he was working at a store selling watches. I could be wrong, but I believe that was probably the only job that he ever had. I never minded having to give him a ride to or from work. I would have done it every chance I could if it meant keeping him out of trouble. That was the first time I had ever seen that he was actually trying to do something positive with his life, just like DeJohn did when he turned to the Nation of Islam. Although he probably wasn't making much money selling watches, I was proud of him. I remember how "hyped" he was as we sat there and listened to the song over and over again as he laughed the entire time. We couldn't believe just how raw Nas was on "Ether."

I often sit back and reminisce about him and the times we spent hanging out. But like many friendships in the streets, we had a falling out just before he ended up getting locked up. I believe he had an issue with someone I was close to and for whatever reason, he felt that we could no longer be friends. I wasn't upset with him about it though. That's just how friendships came and went on the streets. It was either that or fight and kill each other like every other punk did when they felt threatened or offended. Not a day goes by that I don't wish we that we could go back in time to when we were sitting in my car and me being able to push just a little harder to help him change.

Some people just never really stood a chance though. I had my reasons for making the choice to sell drugs. Unfortunately, I believe that he was born right into it. But, knowing somebody personally was totally different from knowing them while they were out there on the streets. Behind the scenes, many of the hustlers I knew were very smart, but in front of others, no weakness could ever be shown, especially when you were always known as a "thug". You had to protect that rep as much as possible to keep anyone from testing you. The sad part about having a certain reputation was that you even had to be careful who you smiled in front of because you didn't want them to think you were soft. That explains all the poses and "mean muggin" when we took pictures; we all lived a double life.

I used to really enjoy hanging out with him. I was probably one of the few people that ever got to see a different side of him. I will never forget having that one on one with him that day and telling him that I really believed in him. I told him that he had already been through enough and needed change before anything happened to him. He looked at me as if I were speaking an entirely different language to him. It was probably the first time anyone had ever given him any positive advice. Everyone else just saw a thug; I saw a friend. Unfortunately, nothing can help change where he is at right now.

I wished he would have listened to me. I sometimes wonder if a thought of that conversation that we had ever crosses his mind. He's one of the main reasons why I decided to change. It was that conversation that made me realize that the longer any of us continued out on the streets, the greater we ran the risk of something negative happening to us. I didn't want to end my days in the streets being a victim or an inmate. Again, I was very lucky to never have to suffer being either one. Most of the stories I share usually end up with a victim. This one ends with a really good friend of mine doing life in prison. I hope that this book ends up in his hands one day so that he knows just how much I really did care for him. I wish things would have turned out better than they did for him.

STICK BALL

Losing someone who you always saw or stood next to day in and night out was tough. I never wanted to see anyone get shot, let alone die over something stupid. Just knowing that you will never see them again was very hard to accept. Even if it was someone that you really didn't associate with much, you knew that they were at least loved by someone. But, if you know anything about the streets, you knew that everything and everyone was really unfortunate and unpredictable. One minute we were all laughing together and the next, you would be crying over their body in a casket. As for me, I honestly have lost count of how many people have been killed out there in the streets of New London. For some, killing was just part of the game. Here's an example as to just how easy and how fast these situations occurred.

On this particular day, I was standing on the same corner where that July 4th weekend shooting had taken place. My cousin Rene and I were just sitting on his porch having a few beers and smoking Black and Milds when we decided to play stick ball in the middle of the street. I grabbed the tennis ball, he picked up a stick that we used as a bat and we just started having a little fun trying to strike each other out. After a few pitches, I had to pause our game because to my right, I noticed three guys coming my way. I knew all three of them, but you just never knew people's intentions. For bragging purposes, yes, I was carrying a gun. I had my permit, so I always kept a gun on me. You might be asking yourself, "Well, why is this idiot carrying a gun and playing stick ball at the same time?" Looking back, you could be right, perhaps it was not such a bright idea I guess, especially after having a few beers. But, where I was from, you couldn't trust anyone. I carried a gun every single day after Babe got killed. Putting my hands up to fight a fair one was no longer an option for me after that.

I noticed that they were taking their sweet time crossing the street, so I began to think that something was about to go down. The closer they got, the closer my hand got to my gun. It was a small .22 so I would have had no problem struggling to get at least one shot off if I had to. So, as they approached, I heard one of the kids say to the other two, "Keep walking, I'll catch up to you guys in a few." So now I'm definitely confused. He comes up to me and asked, "Can I talk to you for a minute?" Now mind you, the next morning I was supposed to be heading down to Tampa. But the way that it was beginning to feel, it was more like I was going to end up dead or on the run somewhere in New York. So, I replied, "Yea, what up?" He says, "I've been hearing a lot of good things about you and how you've changed ever since you left the streets alone. I'm trying to do the same thing," he says. "What made you change?" he asked.

Confused, I'm stuck standing there because I wasn't expecting him to stop and talk to me in the first place. I made sure I kept an eye out for the other two kids and also paid a lot of attention to where his hands were going every second that he stood in front of me. I didn't really trust him or the situation. In my thoughts, I'm thinking this kid was going to either try to rob or shoot me because him and I weren't friends in any way. The entire time he stood in front of me, my right hand was in my pocket holding on to my gun in case he tried to do anything stupid. Then he says, "I know that you have been on the streets most of your life and I heard that you were writing a book about it. How were you able to make that change?" I was surprised because I had never really told anyone I was writing a book.

The only ones that knew that at the time were a few of my relatives and that's only because they always saw me on my computer all day and night. So, to answer his question, I simply just told him the same thing everyone used to always try to tell me. I said to him, "You see those two guys that are waiting for you up the street?" He replied, "Yea, what about them?" I said, "You need to pick better friends; that would be a great start for you." He just stood there for a few seconds with a blank stare. I'm not sure if he was expecting me to give him this long speech about how to go about it, but I figured I'd just keep it simple. He stood there quietly for a few seconds, then looked to the ground and then back up into my eyes and said, "Thanks, bro." We shook hands and as he slowly began to walk away, he says "We'll talk more later." That was it. He then began jogging up the street to catch up with his two friends.

As soon as he made it half way up the street, I shouted over to my cousin and told him to pick up the stick so we could continue our game. I took another quick peek to make sure that they weren't trying to set me up, but then noticed that all three of them had made it up to the corner and were headed towards the next street over. I'd say about three pitches later, I heard about seven or eight gunshots. My cousin just stared at me and after the shots ended he says, "Those aren't fireworks." As soon as he said that, I dropped the ball, he tossed the bat and we both ran towards the back of his house to hop the fence to go see what had just happened. Once we made it to the other side, which was the street that I actually lived on, I noticed a small crowd up the street. So, I made my way up there just to make sure that it wasn't someone that I knew. And there he was. One minute he was asking me for advice and the next minute he was slowly dying. I closed my eyes for a few seconds and said a quick prayer for him as I walked away from his crying mother and the rest of his family members.

For a second, I was once again stuck wishing our conversation lasted a little longer. This was the third time that I had just been talking to somebody and the next minute they were fighting to take their last breath. Just a few minutes later and he was lying on the sidewalk with about 5 or   6 bullet holes in him. His mother was on one knee next to him and looking at me while screaming and crying for me to help her son out. I was numb. I had already been down this road just a few years prior. And judging by the look in his eyes, I just knew he was about to die. In my thoughts, there was no way that he was going to survive. There was way too much blood and his body was so weak that I honestly felt he had about 10 more seconds to live.

If I remember correctly, this kid was wearing a white t-shirt that day. By the time I hopped the fence and saw him lying on the ground, the entire front of his shirt was soaked in blood and his eyes were slowly beginning to roll to the back of his head. His mother kept begging me to help him, but I honestly thought that he was not going to make it. It reminded me too much of the time when I stood there at Lucky's parking lot watching Todd on one knee holding on to Babe as he died in his arms. I didn't want to go through that again, so I just turned around and walked away from the scene. I felt really bad about walking away but it was just too much for me. I just prayed for him to make it through and for him to become the person he wanted to be.

He and I had never spoken a day in our lives before that although we lived on the same street. In fact, we lived two houses down from each other on Belden Street. I never had any issues with him and really can't tell you why we didn't speak. It was like that out in the streets though. I just found it very strange that on the same day that he decided to speak to me that it would be on the day he got shot. I'm not going to say that by that time I was desensitized after seeing and having been through so much already in my past, but once we got back to the other side, we just sparked up another cigar and started playing stick ball again. It was just my way of continuing on with my life and not allowing another situation to affect me mentally anymore.

To make a long story short, he did survive. After a few days at the hospital, I heard that they took him straight to prison. I believe that while the paramedics were checking him, they found rocks of crack cocaine in his socks. I thought about our conversation prior to him almost being killed and wondered over and over again as to what the purpose and meaning behind this entire situation really was. He was still hanging out with other drug dealers and was still dealing drugs. And then

I remembered how many times I tried to stop selling drugs but never could. I knew that by the way he was speaking to me that he really did want to be a better person. If you ask me, I believe that a person who has smoked their entire life had a better chance at quitting smoking cigarettes a lot faster than a drug dealer would from selling drugs. Selling drugs is also an addiction. No matter how hard you tried letting it go, it just wasn't going to happen overnight.

I haven't seen or heard anything about the kid again since the day he got shot. I just hope that he is doing better today than he was back then. That's just how it was in my neighborhood. One minute everything was peaceful and calm, and the next minute you were left standing there shocked and in disbelief. But, even though we always knew that these things could happen at any time, nothing ever changed. We still continued to hang out there like none of it ever occurred. That's just what we were used to doing. We hated to see anyone get shot or killed, but we weren't just going to stay in the house because of it either. The very next day, I drove down to Tampa.

EL FILIPINO

I remember when I was a kid growing up and wanting to become a cop when I got older. I loved the way the sirens sounded from their police cars, the way the lights flashed, and even the way that their uniforms looked. Of course, that was all due to loving the show Chips back in the day. I wanted to be just like Frank "Ponch" Poncherello. Ponch made being a cop look really cool. The way he made you laugh, the way he dealt with people, the way he carried himself. Till this day, I believe that he was the best cop to ever put on a police uniform. In fact, I believe that they should use some of Chip's episodes at the police academy to help rookies work on their personalities before they begin patrolling the streets.

Those were my dreams as a kid growing up in the early 80s. Fast forward to when I turned 12 and suddenly, I began to dislike police officers. Although I never really had to deal with them in any way personally at that age, I used to see how they would come into our projects and chase those that I looked up to and wanted to be like. One day, I remember sitting on a bench by the A Building when I saw three cop cars pulling in to the parking lot. Out of nowhere, they jumped out and began chasing after some of the dealers that had been hanging out. Out of all the people that ran from them, Babe was the one they caught. He was running up a small hill right behind his building when a female officer caught up to him from behind and tackled him. From that day forward, I hated them all. Just like that.

But I guess it was all the brainwashing from the drug dealers and that N.W.A. song that I would listen to all the time that brought me to that way of thinking. Of course, I no longer feel that way about them today, but as a kid growing up, I didn't know any better. I always remembered feeling safe when Babe and DeJohn were around because they were the ones who kept everyone else who wasn't from Crystal Avenue away. It was much safer and more peaceful when they were there to regulate. So, anytime they were incarcerated, you felt the difference. Although there were many more dealers who would also enforce "Crystal Law," they were the ones people feared and respected the most.

Out of all the cops that would come down and harass us, there was this one undercover officer that everyone knew. He was very popular around the city. He went by the name of "El Filipino." That's what all the Spanish drug dealers in my building used to call him. He was known for putting everyone away. It didn't matter how long you had been selling drugs or how good you were at it, he was always one step ahead of everyone. He didn't need snitches. He would sleep in a dumpster if he had to, just to catch you the next morning. I've even heard stories that he used to dress up as a woman to hide his identity. There wasn't a day that you wouldn't hear his name. There were times that he would just walk through and not even arrest or mess with anyone. He just wanted you to see him walking through. By the way everyone looked at him when he walked through, you would have thought it was Satan.

The very first time that I ever saw "El Filipino" was a crazy experience for me. My dad had just sent me to the liquor store to buy him cigarettes and play the numbers for him. The owner of the liquor store was the sponsor of my dad's softball team, so he never asked any questions. As I crossed the street, El Filipino snuck up on me from behind and threw me up against the brick wall right under our 3rd floor window. I don't know if he thought I was already dealing drugs or because he had seen me hanging out with someone that he had been watching and felt the need to search me. I wasn't dealing at the time but for some reason or another, it made me feel like one of "the boys." Hearing his name every day was like hearing about an urban legend. He was so sneaky that he could be right next to you and you wouldn't even notice him standing there until it was already too late. So, being harassed by him made me feel somewhat special.

El Filipino snatching me up and searching me didn't make me cry or make me nervous. Instead, it just made me want to sell drugs and hang out with all the cool drug dealers that I had just begun to admire even more. The moment he put his hands on me, it sort of had a reverse effect on me. Most people would have feared selling drugs after that, but it actually made me want to do it even more. I heard so many stories about this detective that I felt like I was "known" because I was harassed by him. I didn't think that anyone had seen him frisking me, but all it took was one of the drug dealers who had witnessed it to bring it up in conversation for me to feel like I was "down." As stupid as it may sound, it was something for me to brag about. It was crazy just how much of an impact that detective had on me to wanting to sell drugs instead of making me do the opposite.

Ever since that day, I was dodging police officers for the next 20 years. I considered myself a really good drug dealer because I was always cautious of my surroundings. At least I always thought I was. Other drug dealers on the streets had a better chance of robbing me than a cop did catching me in possession of anything illegal. I barely ever kept anything on me while I hustled. I usually only carried just enough to make a few hundred dollars and then spent the rest of the day getting drunk and hanging out. I was now sitting in the front row of a game that I had been a fan of for so long. Looking back, I can tell you that my decision to sell drugs was really ignorant and stupid. Most people will never understand how "being down" is a great feeling. I'm not promoting or glamorizing that selling drugs is acceptable. But now that I am older, I pray and hope that kids never look at selling drugs and committing crimes as a cool thing to do. Lucky for us, El Filipino wasn't trigger happy cause Lord knows what he and his partners had to go through to put people like us away.

I never really had to run from the police. Anytime that they did come around though, I used to always get mouthy with them. Especially when they were cocky, and I wasn't in possession of anything illegal. Most people thought I was showing off anytime that I talked shit to them, but after so many years of them coming around and ruining "our fun", I decided to make them work harder for their money. Yes, I was that stupid. I never really threatened them, but I did always question them about why they were constantly coming around to fuck with us. In my thoughts, we weren't bothering anybody. So what if people wanted to get high, that was their business. Of course, looking back at my behavior and how the streets made me feel like I was untouchable, I can now answer this question for everyone. Everyone always asks police officers if they don't have anything better to do than to come around and harass us all the time. Well, honestly, the answer is "no." If you're out there selling drugs and being rowdy, it is their job to harass you. You will understand that better when you buy your own home or become a parent. Because I can guarantee you then that you will not like being a victim to the same ignorant things you have always enjoyed doing to others.

Now that I am older, I see why some cops abuse their power. I'm not saying that police officers should go around beating people up or shooting at them, but I want you to picture yourself being an officer and having to work in dangerous neighborhoods and having to do it professionally while we treated them like shit as soon as they approached us. On the flipside to that, I believe that all officers should always try their hardest to remain as calm as possible to try and resolve matters as peacefully as possible. But of course, just like there were assholes like us in the streets, there were even bigger assholes in a uniform. They just had the law on their side. Anything that we did or said was always going to be used against us while mostly everything that they did was justified. So, it's a double-edged situation no matter who feels they are right.

I have come across many great police officers throughout my years on the streets. Yes, some were dicks, but I always understood why in some cases they had to be. I was a drug dealer and I was out there committing crimes, right? Why should I have expected to be treated with respect? I wasn't special in any way, and they had a job to do. If I didn't spend so much time out on the streets like I did, I wouldn't have to worry so much about being harassed, period. We do have the freedom to hang out, but it's what you're doing that's constantly attracting them to you. Back in the day, I would probably spend anywhere between 10 to 16 hours in the projects or on a street corner. But, if it wasn't for our ignorance, there would have been nothing for us to have to be worried about. I just loved the streets that much. I knew that there was always a possibility of them getting out of their cruisers to question me but instead of me trying to figure out why they were harassing me, I was always disrespecting them and being rebellious instead.

There are many crooked cops out there. But there were some who were cool as long as you didn't disrespect them or expected the same treatment when they were working with their partner. In fact, there were times when we used to all sit around and take a break from dealing drugs just to laugh and talk with some of them. I remember when the same two police officers used to come down and patrol Crystal Avenue on foot.

Honestly, they didn't give a shit about what we did. They were both in their sixties and would barely even look our way while patrolling. They would just park their car and take long walks away from where we were dealing at. We knew they weren't there to mess with us. But when they did come closer to us, we never felt the need to disrespect them in any way. We knew that it was just a matter of time before they would go for another long walk. So, we just waited. In the meantime, we just stood around and tossed a football or held onto a tennis ball that we sliced open a bit to stash our drugs in till they left.

That's when I learned to play right along with them. You didn't mess with them and they wouldn't fuck with us. But, those were the good ol' days. On two occasions I remember police officers warning me about raids that were going to be taking place and that I might have a warrant for my arrest. One of those times, in 2002, I had just got done running a few laps around our baseball park at New London High when a police officer saw me walking towards my car. He parked right next to me, got out and started walking towards me. I didn't have anything illegal on me at the time, so I didn't have to try to run or get away from him. He says to me, "I just want you to know that you guys are all being watched." He proceeded to tell me to be very careful about any illegal movements that we made because there was a confidential informant telling on us and everything that we had been doing. At that time, I was only selling weed so I wasn't really worried about it too much. But, everyone else around me was selling cocaine and heroin. But this officer was dead serious, and I couldn't wait to go hurry up to go and tell my brothers about it. He mentioned that every single day they would go into briefing that our names were always at the top of their list.

Once the officer and I parted ways, I made sure I went to meet with one of my brothers to let him know. My brother was so deep into the street game that he didn't even believe me. In fact, his response to me was "he's full of shit, he's just trying to scare us." About a month later, all of us, including my parents ended up in handcuffs. New London police, Connecticut State troopers and the Feds knocked the doors off the hinges to about 15 houses that day. Everything that the police officer tried to warn us about was true. The snitch, who had been arrested on marijuana charges, was facing about six months in prison for violating his probation. He had just served a little time before that and rather than going back in, he decided to just tell on everybody else instead.

At that time, I was very upset. Not because our house had been raided, but because my parents had also been placed in handcuffs. It was the beginning of the end for me and my drug dealing days. I knew then that I had to finally grow up and begin to make better decisions. I was getting too old to be dealing with all that nonsense. A lot had happened between the time that El Filipino frisked me and when this police officer tried to warn me. By that time, I had witnessed many shootings, several deaths and so many of my friends had been locked up or become hooked on drugs. But, none of those things made me want to leave the streets alone.

It wasn't until I was brought downstairs in handcuffs and I saw the look on my parent's faces. It broke my heart. Here they were, my two hardworking parents who never had anything to do with drugs, were handcuffed and sitting at the table and we were just acting like idiots out on the streets. Although that raid happened in 2002, it took me a few more years to finally give up drug dealing for good. By then, I was almost 30 years old.

FROM A DISTANCE

There are many people in this world that have no clue or any idea about the issues that are going on there in the streets of America. All they know is that we have a big drug and gun problem. They may speak about the problems or just hear about them, yet no matter how many politicians get involved or how many arrests police officers make, the problem never seems to go away. In fact, it only seems to be getting worse. Crazy, isn't it? Considering how tight our airport security is and how strict our Coast Guard and military are, somehow, someway, our issues are far worse than any other country on this planet. But, at the end of the day, regardless how these drugs and guns make it into this country, it is still that one person's choice to want to deal and shoot them. Society makes this issue far more complicated to understand or deal with because they seem to want to make the addicts and drug dealers out to be the victims of America's corrupt government. In my eyes, that is not the case. How those drugs and guns make it here through our borders isn't even a thought or a secret. Once they do make it through, no matter the risk, there will always be someone there with their hands out ready to sell and purchase them. The thought of making easy money was our only goal.

If you think that drug dealers are out there complaining or are worried about how dangerous the streets are or how over populated our prison system is, you really have no idea. It is not until they end up incarcerated themselves and they are slowly brainwashed by other prisoners about how all of this is a trap. As soon as those gates open back up and they are released, they will always have the choice to do it all over again. And with the way that our system is set up, with most employers not hiring ex-felons, there is a great chance that they will eventually pick up right where they left off. Working minimum wage jobs was never an option for a drug dealer unless they were forced into finding a job by their parole or probation officer. In fact, I believe that most drug dealers I've known have done more community service hours in their entire life than they have ever punched a clock. Although selling drugs will always put dealers in situations where they will eventually end up getting caught and right back in prison, they love the streets. Prison was the least of their worries. It's all fun and games until they ended up having to fight to stay free or alive.

There is much more to drug dealing than just standing around trying to make money and being flashy. To the average person walking by from a distance, all that they see is a person or a group of thugs hanging out. And all that they really hear or read about are those who get shot or end up in prison. But, get any closer to the action and you'll see that they are doing about 10 different things that you just aren't able to see from the outside. The closer you get, the more you would understand why police officers automatically jumped out with their guns screaming for everyone to get down on the ground. I never blamed them for it. I get it. I was out there. I knew what they had to deal and put up with. If I myself couldn't fully trust everyone and had to fear the same people that I had known all my life who might try to kill me one day, I can only imagine how they felt about wanting to make it back to their loved ones.

Now that I am on the other side looking in, I can better describe what it is like to view these crazy situations as a witness rather than risk being the victim or a suspect. Although I've experienced many situations that at one time or another I bragged about as being fun because of the rush and thrill, I can honestly admit that most of us who have made it out would rather not put ourselves at risk like that ever again. No matter how much I struggle or how easy it would be to get back in and start making money, no one would ever be able to persuade me to even want to hang out in the streets, never mind start selling drugs again. The average person who hears the few stories that are being told are usually only getting a single person's point of view. But like the

Bible, everyone interprets everything differently. All I can do is try to bring you as close as possible to a drug dealer's daily routine. Although these are just my views, I have witnessed many if not all of the possible situations that usually end up making it to front page news. But, just when you thought you had seen and heard it all, there was always something crazier occurring right around the corner.

I have always wondered how many people had to get robbed, shot, stabbed or killed before the drugs that I was dealing made it into my hands. It's kind of like blood diamonds. While most women show them off on their ring finger, someone out there may have lost their entire arm over it. It's the same concept with drugs. The closer you are to the suppliers, the more dangerous it was. You've seen Scarface, I don't need to go into more detail than that. I used to always hear about "the spot" being robbed by stickup kids, which usually only meant one of three things. Someone got killed, someone will eventually end up dead or the drug prices were going to rise. The drug business is no different than the gas prices you see people constantly complain about. Anytime something happened at the top, we always had to deal with and suffer with it on the bottom. And the higher those prices increased, the more violent drug dealers became. Because when they couldn't get drugs from their suppliers, they would stick up and rob anyone who was out there still making money.

Sometimes it got really hard for us to find good quality drugs to sell. Quantity was never the issue. The more we had to pay for it, the smaller we had to cut and package it to try and make a little more profit. There were times when we added a little bit of ivory soap to make it appear like there was more crack in the vial or baggie. But, the addicts became a little smarter after a few times and began asking if they could taste it before buying to make sure it was all good. And that's when I began to see more and more addicts getting beat up out of their shoes. Not only did they usually come up short with the money, they also started to come around demanding to see what we had and whether they were going to buy or not. Some even thought it was a good idea to turn down one dealer and go to the next one instead, which in turn caused many disputes between dealers. After a while though, most of those addicts just ended up unconscious. Not all addicts were punks either; some of them were just as crazy as the drug dealers themselves, if not crazier.

Thinking back, I still remember the first time my dad began to notice that I was starting to hang out with the wrong crowd. A friend of ours that went by the nickname "Nap" was hanging out in the same projects where I was supposed to rob the kid with the 2 kilos. A few days before that, a well-known addict had gotten jumped by a few dealers on Crystal Avenue. I had always known that the addict that got beat up was crazy as hell. The very next day after getting jumped, he just happened to run into "Nap" across the street on State Pier road. Nap had been talking to another friend of ours named Gary, who is Eugene's oldest brother, that was later convicted and sentenced to over 45 years in prison for allegedly shooting a New London police officer who was trying to arrest him on a warrant. Nap said that the addict came around the corner and just shot him even though Nap, till this day, denies ever hitting him while he was being jumped. Nap later told me that he just wasn't paying attention to his surroundings when he had been shot. I remember hanging out in the C Building that morning when two other dealers came running, yelling out that Nap had just been shot by the addict that had been jumped.

This was just the beginning to the many lectures that my dad began to sit me through. The two dealers that came running into the building after the shooting somehow convinced me to ask my dad if he could give them a ride to the hospital. I don't know what the hell I was thinking that day, but I went and asked my dad anyway. As soon as I told him the reason as to why they needed a ride, my dad stared at me for what felt like the longest minute of my life. He was even more pissed because I had put him on the spot as the two dealers stood right next to us waiting for his response. Not wanting to feel like an asshole, he said okay and gave them a ride. On the outside, I felt cool because I was doing something that I knew the dealers would appreciate. On the inside though, I knew that as soon as we got back home that my dad was not only going to beat my ass for putting him in that situation, but also for hanging out with known drug dealers. The worse part about it was that the man that had just shot Nap was also my dad's fishing buddy and good friend. From that day forward, my dad began to pay closer attention to what me and my brothers were doing outside.

After that incident, I began to witness more of these types of situations on a daily basis. In fact, right out of my window, I saw several people get robbed and left with only their socks and boxers on. Many people were forced into giving up their drugs, money or anything else of value. One of the many things I have always said about drug dealers is that not all drug dealers were thugs or criminals. Most of them sold drugs just because it was an easy thing to do. But, if they ever showed any type of weakness or that they didn't have the heart to protect themselves whenever they had to, they would have been picked on until they gave up dealing. Most drug dealers were afraid of getting caught by the cops but what they really feared the most were those who would sneak up on them out of nowhere with a gun or a knife. In many cases, they were given no other choice but to give up everything or else. The harder they fought back, the more they would have been embarrassed and tortured.

The life of a drug dealer seems really simple if you're just passing by. All you really see is the hand to hand exchange between dealers and addicts. Most people never stop to think that dealers also have a family at home. They all had loved ones who really cared about them even though they weren't directly involved in what they were doing. In fact, most of the dealers I hung around with also had kids. They dealt with many personal issues that you barely knew or heard about unless they spoke about it. Many either had warrants, problems with other drug dealers, owed money, were dealing with someone else's wife or girlfriend, were infected somehow, or maybe even tried killing someone the night before as they stood right next to you like nothing ever happened. And these were the types of situations that when they came back to haunt them, everyone in sight could have ended up being a victim of their various wrongdoings. In most cases, the only one really looking out for these dangerous situations to come up is the one who was in fear of it catching up to them. This is the reason why you often hear about so many innocent bystanders getting killed instead of the intended target.

Although many of the people that you see out there are frequently committing crimes, making money was always their main goal. No one wanted to really have problems. No one wanted to lose their life or their freedom. But, most drug dealers usually ended up hating each other for no real personal reasons. It was usually over rumors or over a woman that most ended up fighting or killing each other over. It's easy to get comfortable out there because you always seem to expect every day to be as peaceful as it might have been the day before. But, one mistake could change all of that. In the end, it's the families that ended up paying or suffering the most. They were the ones that got stuck with the tears and all the painful memories.

So, we can all sit around and blame the law, blame the system, blame the environment, and even blame society. But in the end, it's really you, the dealer and criminal, who has the choice to be who and what you want to be. If your decision is to sell drugs and to commit crimes, it's you who will end up having to face many types of negative consequences for it. Knowing that the system is already against you should be your biggest reason not to want to deal with the streets in the first place. No matter who the laws seem to be against or how many of us seem to be profiled, you are only making it easier for them to continue making you their target. The life of crime is not a black and white problem. It's not America's problem. It's your problem once you decide to break the law. Because once you are sentenced in a courtroom or dead in a casket, the focus will be on the next person in line who will suffer the same way. You'll become just a distant memory.

The street life is very attractive to many due to the freedom of people being able to do whatever it is they want to do. It's like a cat and mouse game where the mouse rarely sees the trap. All he pictures himself doing is getting to that piece of cheese and running. Which is no different than a drug dealer out there on the street. They never think about the dangers that surrounds them on a daily basis until it is too late. No matter how "real" they claim to be, most of them do fear the worse. Most of them claim that they can do prison time or are ready to die, but with my own eyes I have witnessed many of them crying while being placed in handcuffs or laying there afraid of taking their last breath.

SCARRED

I spent almost twenty years in the streets selling drugs and I have nothing to show for it. So, was it really worth it? Well, I can't fully say that it wasn't. I guess if it wasn't me that it would be somebody else telling you these stories. The streets never chose me, I chose the streets. There were many days that I could have stopped if I really wanted to. Nobody forced me to stand out there and sell drugs or commit crimes for them. I hated hearing hustlers saying that they didn't know how to do anything else besides being out there selling drugs. Everyone had a choice to do better, including myself. Easy money has caused so many problems for people. Most of who were out there on Crystal Avenue, Da Hill, on West Coit or on Belden Street were the best of the best when it came to my hometown. By that I mean we weren't just going to let anybody come and take over without us putting up a fight. But this game wasn't for everybody and although I did a great job of hiding my fear, I'm very happy that I made it out in one piece.

People say that I was one of the lucky ones. They all say that God has always been by my side. But I can only imagine how much more He would have done for me had I taken a more positive route instead. Because even though He might have been there for me, I don't wish any of the things I've seen and been through on anyone else. I couldn't really write about everything that I went through because a part of me still feels like those things should stay right where they occurred. It's not about me being loyal or feeling like I would be snitching; I have just always been the kind of person who has never seen, heard or said anything about whatever happened out there. It kept me alive this long; why change now?

For anybody that is out there selling drugs or planning on it, please know one thing: you are not in control of anything else other than that one choice. Everything else will eventually be against you and will catch up to you somehow. Don't think that just because you claim you are a thug or own a gun that you will always be able to handle the pressure of the many things that you will have to deal with. I have seen some of the "realest thugs" that none of us would have ever expected to fold under pressure just sit and point at their own friends just so they could make it back home. That popular saying "it's not personal, it's just business" goes both ways in this game. And telling has become part of the business.

I think about my choices of the past and wonder how much more pain my parents would have had to deal with had me or any of my brothers been killed. To all of us, anyone that was killed was only a friend. But I can only imagine the pain that a mother and a father have to deal with knowing that they had to bury their own child. The pain that a sibling has to go through knowing that they will never see their brother or sister ever again. A wife having to explain to their children that "daddy" will never coming home again. Nothing can ever be more painful than losing a loved one.

I used to always hear how people would sit around and brag about what was real and about how tough they were. I used to really believe it when people would say they had your back no matter what. In most cases, it was all just tough talk. But the "realest" thing that I have ever seen didn't come from a drug dealer or a thug. It came from Ms. Beverly, Babe's mother. I must explain this before I give you my reason why. For years, I was stuck having to deal with the pain and the memory as the situation occurred over and over again in my thoughts and in my dreams. Watching Babe being shot and dying right in front of me was the worst thing that I have ever experienced in my life. I hated that man in the blue coat for what he had done. He had no idea about how much Babe meant to us. He had no idea what a great person he was. I felt like a part of me died that night with him.

Years later, I heard that Ms. Beverly had forgiven the man in the blue coat and even began visiting him at the prison. I have to admit, I was confused by that when I first heard about it. Ms. Beverly was highly respected by all of us at Crystal Avenue. People got out of the way and stayed quiet until she made her way through. But her decision to sit down and meet face to face with the person who killed her son was beyond words for me to even try to understand it. To me, that was a beyond human thing to do. It brought a lot of peace to me knowing that if she could forgive him, that we too had to follow in her footsteps and try to find a way to also move forward. Rest in peace, Ms. Beverly. I will always admire you for who you were and what you meant to so many of us.

I think about my friends Noel Morales (Richie's brother), Anthony "Pookie" Strong and Rhonda Exum (DeJohn's brother and wife), Todd Fine (Merrill "Babe" Epp's brother) and I can't even put myself in their shoes to understand the pain that they must have gone through once they were alone in their thoughts. We can all tattoo their names on our body, we can pour out liquor in their memory, and we can sit around and tell stories about them all day long. But they are the ones that have to go to sleep every night knowing that their loved ones were never coming home. It hurts me as I write this just to think about it.

Although we all had a lot of fun out there in the streets growing up, I would have to say that the answer is still no. The street life was definitely not worth it. Unfortunately, there will always be many more to follow that will continue taking the risk just like we all did. Some will end up becoming suspects and some will be the fallen victims. Nothing will ever change the outcome of many of those situations out there in the streets. All endings will always be the same. The only things that changes are the name on a court docket and the names engraved on a headstone.

MAKING THE CALL

Every morning that I wake up, I always wonder where I would be had I made better choices. The decision to sell drugs at such an early age has affected me in so many different ways. Like most drug dealers usually end up, I am left with nothing but the stories. Not that I ever thought I would have become rich, but I never thought that I would have struggled as much as I have mentally. If there is one thing that the street life taught me was that we didn't value anything for what it was truly worth. We had no respect for anything, never mind anyone. Unfortunately, the struggle didn't hit me hard until I was fully done with the streets. Starting over was not easy.

Although I stopped dealing drugs and hanging out on the streets almost fifteen years ago, I still find myself struggling to deal with things like normal people do or should. I have never been to prison, but I can imagine how an inmate can be institutionalized. I've never been a soldier in the military either, but I can see how they can come back from a war suffering with PTSD. I'm not sure if there is a name for what a drug dealer goes through after witnessing so many violent things, but I feel like it has definitely affected the way I think and live.

A good friend of mine, Earl Dudley, the younger brother of both Gary and Eugene, who also grew up at Crystal Avenue couldn't have said it better. I remember having a conversation with him when he stated that "although we may have done a lot of wrong growing up, we truly believed that it was for all the right reasons." He said that "we were to never be ashamed of who we were or what we did, but that we should be proud of the men that we had become." I say that he couldn't have said it better because while we were all going through our toughest moments in life, we did whatever we felt we needed to do to survive. And yes, we could have made better choices, but at that time, we felt those were our best choices. He himself had front row seats and was one of the youngest ones to witness many of the things in that C Building that I have described in this book.

Ever since I decided to want to live a more positive life, nothing seems to have gone right for me. My reactions to many of the things that I deal with are either negative or explosive. I got so used to making my own decisions at such an early age that I struggle with authority in many ways. I have struggled even harder in my relationships with women as well. Everything always either ended up in an argument or having to part ways because I just didn't know how to respond with a simple okay. The same way that I dealt with my issues in the streets was the same way that I dealt with most of my issues at work and at home. That has never gone well for me.

Many drug dealers think that being out on the streets is the struggle. They are so wrong. They have no idea how much more they will have to struggle with learning how to respond differently to things they were used to dealing with violently. In the streets, when anyone pissed you off, you have a choice to either fight them, stab them or shoot them. Those aren't the same choices you will have when you get into an argument with your significant other or with your boss at work. It won't be easy to take orders from your boss, never mind having to live with your wife and kids in the same home when you are mad at them.

Maturity is when you can set aside your pride and ego as a man and be able to deal with matters in a respectful way by avoiding negative consequences. Anything less than that is simply ignorance. Due to all of this negative behavior and all the bullshit that I had put others through, I feel like I have lost so much because of it. It wasn't until I decided that I no longer needed to shut the world out and began to open up to people that they suddenly began to view me differently. Although many may not really care about my personal preferences or even my point of view, I really just wanted to enjoy life a little more than I have in the past.

I'm not going to lie, when I see people suffering after so many years of making others go through shit, it brings me peace knowing that they are now dealing with their worse moments like I had to. It's wrong, and I know that we should never wish bad luck on anyone but sometimes it takes a person to go through their worst moments to understand and accept that everything in life goes both ways.

Towards the end, I began to look back at all the damage that all of us have caused. I also began to think about how many lives have been ruined by drug use, how many people had been incarcerated, and how many have been shot or killed. I had to ask myself, why did I have to go through all of that only to end up wishing that things were different? I can still remember the first time my mother found a pound of marijuana in my bedroom and smacking me across my face for bringing drugs into the house. I reminisce about living at Crystal Avenue and wonder how life would have been had I just continued to follow my dream of becoming a baseball player. Although I regret my decision to become a drug dealer, I wonder if this was just the path that had been created for me. Was it meant for me to witness so many violent acts in order for me to become an author and write about it in hope that it would help save the lives of others from going through what I have been through? I may never know the answer to that question. But, I will say this. I am happy that my parents never had to visit me in a prison or get that phone call in the middle of the night that I had been shot or killed.

Unfortunately, we had to make that phone call once. There was nothing easy about it either. In fact, I couldn't even work myself up to tell my friend's mother that her son had just crashed his car and might not make it. At first, I tried calling his sister on her cell phone, but she didn't pick up. I didn't want to call their home number that late with the bad news. Once again, I was in a situation where I felt like I could have saved someone's life but didn't. Just five minutes before leaving the bar we were at and him taking off in his car, I saw my friend West coughing a few times into a napkin. I remember asking him if he was okay and him just shaking his head and then said "yea, I'm alright." While I was trying to make sure that he was okay to drive, I took my eye off of him for just a few seconds so I could yell over to one of my other friends to hurry up so we could go home. I turned back around to look for West but he had already left.

We all got into our car and drove off. About a half a mile down the road, we saw a man jumping out in the middle of the street for us to stop and help him look for someone that had just crashed into a tree. I looked around and noticed that the front half of the car was on one side of the yard and the back half was under a tree that had fallen on top of it. I immediately ran to the back half of the car and tried lifting it up, but I didn't see or hear anything. As I began walking towards the front half of the car, one of my friends who was with me at the time yelled out "I found him, he's over here!" I began running towards him and couldn't believe that it was my friend West. We immediately checked his pulse, but it was so weak that we knew he wasn't going to pull through. A few seconds later, an Uncasville police officer told us to get out of his way and leave the scene.

Not a day goes by that I don't wish I had asked him for his keys or had given him a ride home. Once I got back into town, I met with his sister Erica to tell her about what had happened to her brother. I think about West almost every single day. Till this day, I still laugh about how he walked across the stage at our high school graduation in 1994. Most of us had button ups and a tie on. Once he got half way across the stage, he stopped, turned towards the crowd and opened up his gown while only wearing just a pair of boxers and a wife beater tank top. The entire crowd just went crazy after that. He was the last person that I had seen alive just minutes before they passed.

If you've read Loser and Lie'f, you will now understand why I have always felt like the Angel of Death has always circled around me. I'm not sure if he was always after me to be a witness to all these situations so I would change my ways or not. I decided to write this book for two reasons. The first reason of course was to keep my friends' memories alive and for their loved ones to know how much they really meant to me. They were always great people regardless of how anyone may have felt about them. The other reason was so that I can finally begin to let them rest in peace along with finding peace within myself. I've been holding onto them for so long and think about all of them almost every single day because I live with the guilt of wishing I would have done something to protect them and kept them alive. I myself have not lived in peace for many years. Writing this book has definitely helped me to heal in many different ways. I hope that I can now begin to move forward both mentally and physically and finally enjoy my life like I once did.

ACKNOWLEDGMENTS

As I sit here with tears in my eyes, I want to say that as much as I wish that I hadn't been a witness to so many tragic events throughout my life, I believe deep in my heart that this was the way God wanted it to be. I can no longer live with regrets or wish that I could go back and change any of it. I hope that this book reaches the hands of our young children and helps them understand that they do not have to go through what I and so many other people have already been through. There is so much more to life than attention, popularity and material things. No matter how hard times get, please understand that the streets will only make things worse for you. It will temporarily appear like all of your answers will come from money and from all of the people that you will come across, but in the end, it's you who will have to deal with all of the consequences of that lifestyle choice.

Many of you will never understand how I feel deep inside, but I hope that this book somehow helps you make better choices in life. It is very unfortunate that everything that I saw had to happen for me to be able to write this book. There is not a day that I don't think about my past with a heavy heart. I now have sons that I have to raise in this world. I pray God helps me as a father to guide them through a much better life than the one I have lived. They deserve it all.

To all the adults who still are or were once friends of mine, don't take what I have written as being a hypocrite of the things we once did together. Yes, we all loved and enjoyed the street life at one point or another. But I know that none of us, as parents, would ever wish that our own children took that route. This book is very personal, and it does hit home in many ways. I am just trying to help save the lives of our sons who may never be as lucky as we were to make it out.

I want to thank a very close friend of mine who was always in my ear preaching to me every chance he could to help me see things differently in life. Had it not been for Alvin Young, I can honestly say that I would probably be dead or in prison. Thank you for always being there and never giving up on me. I know that I gave you hell, but I want to thank you for bringing peace into my life. Without your advice, I would still be lost. Thank you for your patience.

To my parents, there are no words that could ever describe how much I love you both. I am sorry for all that I have put you through. I know that reading this book will bring back a lot of memories, but I wanted you to know and understand what I went through in my darkest moments. I always wanted the both of you to read about what I was never able to express through conversation. I chose a different path than the one you tried to lead me to, and I am sorry for that. I wish I would have listened. In the end, I know you did all you could for me, and I see and appreciate it now. I've realized it's never too late to right your wrongs in peace.

To Richie Morales, DeJohn Strong, Merrill "Babe" Epps, and Daryl West and to the many others who have fallen victim to the street life, may you all Rest in Peace

Till we all meet again …